HOW TO BE SINGLE

The definitive guide to Singleness

Omotayo Adeola

ISIOMA·S·O

Dedication

To my Best Friend –
Thank You for teaching me Love
and giving me the opportunity
to make You proud.

Table of Contents

Valentine's Day

It was February 14th 2017, and Social Media was really getting on my nerves. On the one hand, there were couples who proudly showed off their flowers, chocolate, surprise singers and all other forms of evidence to show that they were loved, admired; wanted. On the other hand, there were the Fierce Feminists who didn't need a man and, anyway, Valentine's Day was just an over commercialised capitalist scheme. Then there were the encouragers: married people who admonished single ladies not to feel the pressure of the day.

"Your single season is the most important time of your life. Find your purpose, seek God more and enjoy this time," they said, while thanking their husbands for being the best thing to have ever happened to them. But, "don't feel lonely today, Jesus loves you, everyday!"

The lovebirds were annoying but the encouragers were the worst.

I remember talking to one of my friends on the phone, "These people end up making single people feel guilty for feeling lonely!" I ranted. "Going on about how we should 'focus on our purpose' up and down the place. Well, what about those of us who have found our purpose and are already close to God? What about single people who are thriving in their single season already? Why can't we be content with our lives and still want to be married? Why does everyone act like feeling lonely is something to be ashamed of?"

"Mmh," she replied.

"Does anyone tell a woman who really wants to get a good job that 'she is complete in herself' and doesn't need a better job? Does anyone tell a woman who has been trying for a baby to 'keep working on her character and enjoy her married-without-children years'? Of course not! Then **why** do we continue shaming single people for desiring marriage?"

"So true," my married friend said.

"I feel like I have so much to say about being single," I sighed.

"Then you should talk about it!"

"Yeah," I muttered.

But I was afraid.

If I started to talk about singleness, I would have to put myself out there. Not only that, wouldn't I have to remain Single in order to be a true authority on the matter? And I didn't want to be Single, anymore. I was so tired of being strong, being fine, being alone.

It feels like I've wanted to be married since I was born. I'm the only girl in a family of four brothers and two parents and I grew up okay; I had food to eat, clothes on my back and school fees were paid, but there was always an ache in my heart that I eventually filled with the imagination of marriage.

I stumbled on one of my mum's Mills and Boon romance novels when I was eight, and the steamy passion of forbidden love made the ache deepen; the love stories painted the picture of the possibility of *something* that could cure my heartache. The characters seemed to know exactly how I felt; they would fall in love and exclaim some version of, "All my life I've been searching for something... I didn't know what it was, but now I've found it in you."

That's it, I reasoned, I just needed to find this love and it would cure my loneliness!

I became hungrier for romance novels and they painted picture after picture of the many different ways I could hope for the hole in my heart to be filled, but I was also heartbroken in advance as I realised – Nigerian men don't buy flowers or have witty conversations and flirtatious banter. At least, I had never seen my parents do any such thing. As far as I could see, it was all, "Mummy, is food ready?" and "Tell your daddy he has a visitor," between them. That made me cry even more, and I decided that I would have to find a way out of the country to find my perfect Italian heir who was taking a break from the pressures of his fabulous life (because his wealthy parents were trying to force him to marry a woman he didn't love).

He would find me, an unlikely Nigerian with strange hair and a beautiful heart and we would fall impossibly in love, then he would break up with me because it could never be... But, weeks later, he would walk into the art gallery or bookstore I work at and confess that it was only with me that he had ever felt truly alive, and he would risk his fortune for true love.

Then, when I was fifteen, I met a guy. He was witty and intelligent and even thought it was cool to buy flowers (even though he never did buy me any) and I realised I could find Italy right here. The guy broke my heart, *sha*, but that was just a small price to pay for the realisation that my dream could actually come to pass in Nigeria. I would eventually meet other guys, get my feelings hurt over and over, while still waiting for The One who would make all the heartache worth it.

But heartache is never "worth it".

I remember one guy I dated who kept me physically close but was completely distant emotionally. Whenever I would ask what the status of our relationship was (you know, the, "what are we doing?" conversation), he would sigh condescendingly and roll his eyes, "We're together, I like you, you like me. We don't need it to be official," he would say. But when anyone else asked him if he was seeing anyone, his answer was no. Of course, it would get back to me and I'd confront him, "So-and-so said you denied me."

He would sigh again, "You know I don't like people knowing my business. Everyone who's important knows about you."

Listen, this is a scam, and it is still very much alive and active. The "important people" are the ones he can ask to watch his back while he goes around doing whatever else he wants to do. These "important people" are his guys and they're fully aware of all his shady business. There's a bro-code: something like, "Thou shalt pretend that every woman is important, as long as thy bro require-reth it."

PS: Sometimes, family members are the most dangerous "important people".

Every babe that's with such a guy will get the same lines: "Babe, let's just keep this between us." "My guys really like you." "My mum said I should say hi," and yet, it means nothing.

Many years after I had been scammed, I inadvertently found myself acting as one of the "important people" in someone else's scam. This babe had been "with" this guy for a while, almost a year. She thought they were committed.

One day, we were hanging out: my friend, this babe, my friend's brother and I. We were sharing funny stories from past experiences and I was talking about this Top Secret relationship scam.

"Any guy who doesn't take you to public places on dates is dodgy," I shared. "If you only hang out with, like, his brother or best friend but he doesn't take you out or introduce you to his colleagues, run!"

Then she said, "I've never met his friends! Just you guys."

"No, I'm sure you've hung out with them," I laughed, dismissing it.

"No, seriously," she giggled, "Just you guys!"

And that's when I realised I was an accessory to his crime.

My friend, the smooth operator, laughed and pointed out the times they had travelled together or something seemingly important like that, and we changed the topic.

Later, when I accosted him with it, he boldly asserted, "I haven't asked her out, so, whatever."

"Do you plan to?"

"I mean, it's not necessary."

He was getting everything he wanted and she was happy. What was the worst that could happen?

Listen, ladies, just because he has met your parents and you've met his siblings doesn't mean he's actually

11

serious. Lawyers will tell you: only a verbal or written agreement is valid. An assumption based on "but we hang out all the time" is a scam.

But I'm getting ahead of myself.

Despite how much I desired marriage, it just didn't happen. The guys I wanted to marry didn't want to marry me, and I didn't want to marry the one who wanted to marry me.

Sometimes, I lay in bed and wondered whether it was possible to dissolve from loneliness. Like, just disintegrate into a pile of dust and be blown away by the wind. I can be spectacularly dramatic when I choose to let my emotions lead my thoughts. And yet, the weird thing is that none of this showed on the outside. Of course, I moaned about being single with my friends – until they all got married – but I was never that person who asked everyone to hook her up. I went out a lot – weddings, parties, etc. – but I was never the one who made eye contact and flirted confidently.

One of my guy friends said to me, "You act like you're not single," which I took as a compliment, at first, but then I started to wonder... You know how it is when you go out, and you see the lads checking out the ladies and the ladies smiling coyly back, batting their lashes suggestively even without saying a word? Or when a babe "takes a walk" around a party to "look for her friends" but she walks slowly – by herself? Well, I walked too fast. I laughed and chatted with the people I already knew and, for the life of me, I still don't know how to bat my lashes. I acted like I was out with my friends rather than out on the prowl. My "Single" signal was a confusing Amber and I didn't know what to do about it. I didn't know whether I was supposed to do anything about it.

I felt confident when I was out and I loved to dance, but I always went home disappointed when I didn't get chatted up; another full face of make up and carefully chosen outfit wasted, yet again. And then the few guys who would occasionally take my number wouldn't call.

Was there something wrong with me? Even if it wasn't, like, wrong *wrong*; maybe just a little off. Maybe I was just a little weird. Maybe I wasn't sexy enough. After all, my ex had told me I had "the bum of a white woman". Maybe, maybe, maybe.

There's this common saying, "there's a hole in everyone's heart that only God can fill." Whenever I'd come across it I'd think to myself, that doesn't even make any sense; God is too big to fit in a hole. And even if there really is such a thing, then the fact that there's *a* hole for God doesn't mean it's the *only* hole; pretty certain there are many holes in our hearts that many different things are meant to fill. I mean, I had a marriage-shaped hole *and* a money-shaped hole I was trying to fill, and if God wanted a hole of His own, fine by me, but He could go ahead and fill it up by Himself.

Furthermore, this whole marriage thing, *sef*; people didn't really look happy in it. Wives were always complaining about their husbands and threatening to leave, because, "We're not in the olden days anymore and a woman doesn't need her husband to make ends meet. I don't have to take it from him!"

Men also stopped trying to be romantic, lost interest in their wives after they'd had a few babies and generally thought they were doing the women a favour by staying with them. Some men bragged that they were good husbands because they were discreet. "No, I can never disrespect my wife by cheating in her face for everyone to see. I keep it away from home."

Aunts advised, "See, all men are the same. Just find one you can manage and close your eyes."

A married man once told me that he loved his wife, but he just had a weakness (for other women) and she understood him. *Whatever works for you*, I thought, but if these were my only options, they were extremely bleak.

But I couldn't understand: if marriage was a bed of private misery and public pretence, why were these very same unhappy men and women trying to encourage me to enter into it?

"Ah, no, but marriage can be really sweet," someone would say, in-between complaining about her husband.

(It really seemed like the women were perfect and the men were the ones with the problem.)

What was even more ridiculous was that, even after everything I had seen, heard and learnt about the darn thing, that achy hole in my heart was still dreaming of finding one who would defy all the odds in the universe and actually fill it with love.

I was ashamed of this persistent desire to be married. I mean, I knew better than to tie my hopes and dreams to the conformist idea of a union between a man and a woman that, statistically, was fifty percent likely to end in tears and regret. It felt as if desiring marriage meant that I was not a strong woman; that I was breaking the feminist ranks and giving my power away to a member of The Patriarchy.

And, yet, every Valentine's Day, I would find myself, single, alone and unwanted, dreaming of the day I would also become an encourager:

"I used to be like you, wishing someone would complete me. Then I found out that no one can complete you but God! PS: thank you for the flowers, baby! You're the best and I love you. Happy Valentine's Day! x."

Fruits and Broomsticks

My favourite analogy for Singleness involves comparing Fruits to Broomsticks. I'll explain:

When we're single, most of us feel incomplete, like we're lacking something. The same way a broomstick that's separated from the bunch is useless to sweep, we feel like we're lacking something or some*one* and, until we are joined together with that person, there's only so much we can do on our own.

One day, I decided to look up the word, "Single" in the dictionary. As expected, it was linked to all the negative feelings of loneliness, being separated and isolated, with the weight of lack hanging over it. "Single" and lonely… "Single" and lacking a partner… "Single" and incomplete… I knew that couldn't be right.

I eventually found a synonym that painted a more accurate picture: the word "Whole." "Whole", meaning, a thing that is complete all by itself.

Where a single broomstick is isolated, lonely, ineffective, incomplete and separated, a single fruit is whole: it is complete in itself. A single fruit has all the juice and nutrients it needs. A single fruit has enough seeds to create a forest; it carries in itself everything it needs to multiply. It is **whole**.

And so the first thing to understand about Singleness is that you are whole. You are not lacking anything; everything you need is inside you. You do not need another person to be complete, you do not need another person to be effective, and you do not need another person to make you valuable. You do not need another person to validate you and make you feel wanted, loved and special. You are all that, all by yourself.

"... Perfect and complete, lacking nothing." James 1:4 (NIV)

But I know you don't really believe that, not deep down in your heart when you're alone with your thoughts and feelings. You know how to say the words, how to share the quotes online, how to square your shoulders and dress the part, but you still think there's something missing. Like me, every time you think of your singleness you wonder if it's possible that there's something wrong with you – maybe it's the way you dress? Maybe your job doesn't allow you to socialise? Maybe you need to change your hairstyle?

You've heard that guys like girls who think and behave a certain way and you wonder, maybe you just don't have it. You're not sure if it's because you have a character flaw or if it's just how you were born and, sometimes, you think it's just how life is: doing the best you can, day by day, but never truly feeling fulfilled.

Of course, you're intelligent enough to understand that relationships aren't everything. You know that there's more to life. You didn't need a man to achieve any of the amazing things you've been able to achieve... but it would be nice to find someone to share life with. You know that marriage isn't everything but you hope it can be something... something special.

Years ago, one of my friends said to me, "Do you think anyone is really happy? What if what you think is happy is different from what they think is happy?"

I argued back, "The fact that people don't know they're unhappy – or don't say they're unhappy – doesn't mean they're happy."

"Who are you to judge who's happy or not? What if they don't want more from life? What if they've never known anything else, and how they are is enough for them?"

"Everyone wants to be treated well," I insisted.

"But, what if your standards are different from theirs?"

"The fact that they're okay living their lives like that doesn't mean they're happy with it."

"But how do you know they're not? Who are you to impose your standards on them?"

Of course, we were arguing about different things, even though it sounded the same. It's like apples and oranges; they're both fruits and they're both nutritious but they are not the same. You have to peel the skin of an orange to get to the juice, but you can eat an apple as it is. I was talking about the universal need to be valued, affirmed and loved; she was talking about how we *measure* value, affirmation and love.

We often mix the two up. It's true that people have different needs, different perspectives and different expectations from life – and from love; one person thinks love is being able to sit in companionable silence, but another person thinks that being able to talk for hours is the greatest measure of love. It would be wrong to expect love to look one certain way. Most of our parents and grandparents did not go on candlelight dinners and perhaps the most romantic thing they ever said to each other was, "Have you eaten?" but that doesn't mean they didn't love each other deeply.

The fact that love has different expressions is one thing and the fact that everyone needs love is another. I believe that everyone needs love in order to feel fulfilled.

We search for it in our jobs, in our faith, in our community service, in our romantic relationships, in our children, in our friends, everywhere. We don't even know if it exists, but we instinctively hope for it. Isn't that the biggest mystery of life?

And now these three remain: faith, hope and love.
But the greatest of these is love. (1 Corinthians 13:13
NIV)

But, if this is true, what *is* love?

Love is...

I was dating a guy, once. Nice guy, really sweet, etc.
One day, out of the blues, he said he loved me.

Ha.

We were just hanging out as usual, nothing special
had happened. So what, I liked him, too – maybe even a
lot. Maybe I had even told him that he was the best
boyfriend ever. It's possible that I had told him I cared
about him and I was really happy with him. It's likely
that I enjoyed spending time with him, too, that my face
lit up every time his name popped up on my phone, that
I ran to hug him whenever we hadn't hung out in a few
days as if he was returning from the battlefront, or
something. And so? Is it just that little affection that
warranted this declaration? I mean, love?

I sat there, o. I didn't know what to say. I think I
hugged him and made a weird sound, something like,
"aww". I mean, I didn't want to be rude and say thank
you. What was a girl to do?

The moment was ruined. There was no salvaging
this mess. He dropped me at home. I panicked, was he
going to break up with me because of this?! See, this

was exactly why we didn't need to get into all this love, stuff; why ruin a perfectly happy relationship with such a wrecking ball of an announcement? Who asked you, sir? Why couldn't you keep it to yourself?

I didn't want to lose him and I didn't want to hurt him and I could *not* say I loved him, back. I had to find a way to do something about this... situation.

"But we have talked about this, ehn," I said to myself as I paced in my room.

And we had. I had let him know very clearly that I believed that saying the L word was essentially a marriage proposal. We were quite young so I'd said that to scare him a bit, make him really take his time and watch his words around me; just because we were lovey-dovey didn't mean we were in love or anything like that. I didn't allow myself to consider that he might have been fully aware of what he was saying.

"Impossible. We're not there, yet," I convinced myself, but I still didn't know what to do to contain this love-leak.

"What is love, *sef*?" I asked, angrily.

I didn't know, but I was a Destiny's Child fan and I remembered that Michelle had quoted a bible verse in one of their outros, and the verse talked about love, so I looked it up:

Love is patient, love is kind. It does not envy, it does not boast, it is not proud. It is not rude, it is not self-seeking, it is not easily angered, it keeps no account of wrongs. Love takes no pleasure in evil, but rejoices in the truth. It bears all things, believes all things, hopes all things, endures all things. Love never fails. (1 Corinthians 13:4-8 Berean Study Bible)

Well, this was a problem. My guy was patient and kind. He wasn't proud or rude or selfish. What was all this?

Then he called me, disappointed by my lack of response.

I argued, "Listen, it's not that I don't care about you, it's just that I think that word is really strong. What does it even mean? Is it, like, a strong like you feel? Maybe not quite love…"

"You can't really tell me what I feel," he started, and, of course, he was right. And angry.

So I said, "Wait, so I went to look up love. First Corinthians. And I realise you are all these things to me. I really care about you, I may even feel it back, I just can't say it. Is that okay? Can you understand?"

"Wow," he said, speechless, "First Corinthians, huh."

I didn't realise what I had just admitted to, but he did.

As I looked back at this experience, I see one glaring signpost that points to fear. I was so afraid. I didn't know I was. I was afraid that love was an illusion, that it didn't last, that it didn't mean anything. I was afraid that someone could say they loved you, today, and hurt you, tomorrow. I was afraid that love meant that I would want to be with one person for the rest of my life, and that he would have the license to hurt me for the rest of my life and I would be stuck there, unable and, perhaps, even unwilling to leave, because I loved him so much.

Love was so fickle, too; well, the word was. I believed that true love was special and rare; yet, everyone kept throwing the word about as if it had no weight. Real love, I was certain, was a heavy, weighty thing that pulled on you like the center of gravity until you could only be with the one, singular person in the world that you loved. And in the same way you can only ever have one center of gravity, I believed you could only ever truly love one person.

I thought I had felt that way, once, but the guy had lied to me and so I decided that it had just been my imagination and I kept it moving. I even made up a quote, something like, "You can only have you heart broken once; every other time, it was your pride."

As dramatic as my definition of love is (I mean, the center of gravity?) the funny thing is that it's sort of true. It is a hundred percent true about God and, if God is Love, then it is also true about love. However, it is not at all true about romantic feelings – which we sometimes call love.

The problem is that we often mix up our desire for God's love with our desire for romantic love. God's Love is the center of gravity of our entire lives: it is in Him and because of Him that we are alive, it is because of Him that we can experience life, good health, thriving careers and even romantic love, and it is because of him that we have such distinct and diverse personalities, preferences, desires, appearances and identities.

Romantic love is one of the many expressions of love that we can experience, but it is not the only expression of love there is. In fact, there is a different expression of love that is tied to every one of our major relationships.

There's the love of a mother. It is similar to, but different from the love of a father. There's the love of a sibling, which is similar to, but different from the love of a close friend. There's the love of a colleague, of a mentor, of a minister in church, and on and on. For every aspect of life, there is a relationship. For every relationship, there is an expression of love or, let's use the word, "value", that can be experienced. Each one of those contact points is an opportunity to experience love in a different way.

Culture and society tend to dismiss the necessity of love outside of the family. If you're not related and you're not dating, it is almost seen as childish to expect value and love from any other relationships, but I believe that human beings were wired to need love – both to give and to receive it – from every major human contact point.

I believe Love can be defined as Value: the value God places on us, the value we place on ourselves and the value we place on the people around us.

Value is measured by sacrifice. In Economics there's the concept of the Opportunity Cost, which is defined as "the loss of other alternatives when one alternative is chosen." If you choose to take up a 9-5 job in Bank A, you have given up the potential of the job in Bank B. If you choose to date Person A, you have given up the potential of Person B. When you make choices like that, you factor in all the alternatives and decide that this one thing is worth them all.

"...The Kingdom of Heaven is like a pearl merchant on the lookout for choice pearls. He discovered a real bargain—a pearl of great value—and sold everything he owned to purchase it!" (Matthew 13:45-46 TLB)

Choosing the pearl meant giving up everything he owned. He sacrificed "everything he owned" to buy one pearl – that was the value he placed on the pearl.

We don't always recognise or accept the value God places on us – and in us – but it's there, regardless. He gave up His life in exchange for ours – that means He is saying our lives are as valuable as His. That is what "for God so loved the world…" means. He values us as much as He values His own life.

Because we struggle to accept the value God has placed on us, we struggle to value ourselves. We neglect our physical and mental health, we don't like our bodies, we don't value our gifts and talents, we compare ourselves to others and feel unworthy. However, because we are innately worthy – as in, we are made of God, made from God and made for God, we are valuable and worthy whether we realise it or not – therefore we constantly keep feeling like there must be more to life. That hunger, that desire, that search for meaning, it comes from a place of believing that we were meant for more. We don't always know what that "more" looks like, we still struggle with insecurity and shame, but something in us continues looking for value, love, affirmation from *something*.

That *something* is the feeling of being incomplete that many of us singles feel.

We think we're looking for love. We think we're lonely because we're not in committed relationships. We think the tears and the frustrations and the repeated heartbreaks are the problem, that the companionship that comes with marriage is the solution.

We are wrong: the reason we feel incomplete is that we have not learnt to value ourselves, to love ourselves, to affirm ourselves.

We want other people to love us so that we'll finally believe that we are worthy of love, but it doesn't work. You can't love someone enough if they don't love themselves first.

If you've ever been in a relationship where you gave and gave and gave but it was never enough for the other person, it's because you were pouring your love into someone who didn't believe they were worthy of love, so they either couldn't receive your love or they couldn't reciprocate it. These dysfunctional situations come up a lot in relationships when we are not confident in our worth.

Here are a few Dysfunctional Love Languages to look out for:

Scenario 1: The Needy Lover

This person needs you all the time. "Why do you like me?" "Why haven't you called me?" "Where are you?" "I thought we were going to hang out!" "Please don't leave me." "Tell me again, why you like me?"

At first it feels nice to be needed and wanted so much, but in the end you feel drained. It's never enough. You can do everything for them and they'll still feel like you don't love them enough.

The love you're pouring into them is draining out through them like water in a sieve.

Scenario 2: The Brick Wall

This person barely communicates, doesn't want to address issues, deflects when you try to get deep. They may be very physically expressive, intensely sexual, that sort of thing; but it's hard to get them to express their feelings, because they don't allow themselves to acknowledge that they have any.

Scenario 3: The Over-Lover

This person does *everything* and more. They give their life for the one they love – even when it is clear that it's not reciprocated.

"Just give me a chance; I can love you enough to prove myself to you." "I know you're not ready to commit, but I will love you so much that you'll realise you want to be with me."

They take on every fault, dismiss every mistake and apologise for the other person's wrongdoing because it is important for them to be the most loving and most forgiving.

They give love with the hopes that it will prove that they're worthy to receive love.

Scenario 4: The Vampire

This person drinks up all the love they get – and doesn't feel the need to reciprocate. They are excellent at receiving love and they know how to extract it when they want it. They are confident about their ability to get love and pride themselves on it, but they don't feel the need to give love.

The principle of love in the bible depicts the idea of being filled up until we overflow, so that we have enough to give without emptying ourselves.

Needy Lovers don't have the capacity to hold on to love: they're more like baskets than buckets.

Brick Walls are like buckets turned upside down: they cannot receive; love bounces off them.

Overlovers are constantly draining themselves; pouring themselves out in the hopes that they will be able to convince someone else to pour back into them.

Vampires take what they need and stop there – they don't need any overflow because their focus is on themselves.

This is a good place to pause and assess: which one are you?

"You Don't Know How To Receive Love"

It was a few days after my twenty-fourth birthday. My boyfriend of two and a half years and I had just broken up, but I hadn't told my parents. My mum came up to me where I sat and said, wistfully, "Your next birthday is on a Saturday. Perfect wedding date."

That was when I realised she needed to know it was over.

A few days after I told her, I woke up in the middle of the night to find her at the foot of my bed.

"When you told me you broke up, I cried and cried."

"Why? You didn't even know him," I retorted.

Truly, she hadn't. I had never invited him for a family event. He had never spoken to any parent or sibling for longer than a couple of seconds on his way in or out of my house on the very rare occasions I opted to hang out at home – and I mean, like, twice. He never spoke to any family member on the phone. They'd never bonded, shared jokes or plans for the future.

My parents had never known about any of my relationships until this one and, if I had known how hard they would take the breakup, I would have kept it hidden, as well. I had clearly underestimated the power of their desire to see me married.

Again, if I had known.

My dad summoned me to his study a few days after. I didn't know what to expect. I figured we would have an intellectual discussion about pros and cons, something vague and uncomfortable but enough to answer whatever questions he might have had, but nothing more.

I was wrong.

It started off intellectual, yes, but ended with me gasping out my replies to his questions between sobs, trying to catch my snot with my hands because I had run out of tissue, as he scolded me for my inability to make good decisions. He finished me off with the gut-punching declaration, "You don't know how to receive love!"

I left his study hurt, angry and disappointed in his approach to fatherly concern.

"What kind of nonsense is that, 'I don't know how to receive love'!" I fumed – to myself, of course – but that singular statement became like the emotional equivalent of Barney from *How I Met Your Mother*'s Slapsgiving: it was the gut-punch that would keep on punching for the next decade.

Every time I found myself lonely or hurting or any other less-than-optimal emotion, it would hit me again, "Omotayo, you don't know how to receive love."

How does a person receive love, anyway? With a bucket? With a fake smile? With a ring on their finger to prove that someone had finally found them worthy of love?

Doesn't the expression "receive love" suggest that someone must be giving it, in the first place? If so, where were they? Where was I supposed to go to find all the love I was supposed to receive? Who was handing it out?

Furthermore, what did love even mean? What did it look like? How was I supposed to recognise it if it came my way? Did I miss the class where they taught this vital piece of information? Because I was clearly missing something.

I had no idea what love was; how was I supposed to know what it looked like when it tried to stay? But, more importantly, how was I to know that love – if it really had been love – wasn't strong enough to stay even when I tried to push it away?

I argued and argued with my dad in my head but I could never come to the conclusion that his assessment was wrong. I was a Brick Wall, but I didn't realise it. I knew how to communicate and I enjoyed talking so, because I appeared to be open, I didn't realise that I was incredibly guarded.

If you're like me, you have a lot of valid and logical reasons for rejecting love. You understand divorce statistics. You feel desire or loneliness but you are practical enough to put it in a box, to be opened when necessary. You have analysed romantic relationships and have decided that they are simply a necessary evil. You may think it would be nice to love someone, some day, but you're not going to go out of your way to make it happen.

You are confident and self-assured and so you also don't realise that the upside-down bucket of your heart is hiding your vulnerability, your fear of hurt, your fear of losing control. You're afraid that if you give yourself over to love, you'll lose yourself in someone else and you are too strong for that.

Listen, you can't lose your value. It is impossible. The value of a human being is not like the value of currency that can fluctuate when the economy shifts.

You don't have to be afraid.

Value, Currency and God

In its natural state, **Value** is raw, sometimes hidden, and its profitability or usefulness isn't always obvious to the eye. The same way precious stones are buried in the earth, the fact that we can't see how valuable we are doesn't change the fact that we are valuable.

Currency is like a river: it flows when Value is created, used and traded from natural resources. To get gemstones from the ground, we must exert physical energy to mine the earth. To get crude oil, we must exert physical energy to drill thousands of feet into the seabed to extract it.

All of us carry value inside of us. Our gifts and talents are expressions of value that has been deposited in us from God, through our genes, our exposure, our surroundings, our studies, etc.

The money you make from trading with your value can run out, but because the source of your value is God, and God can never run out, your value can never be exhausted.

In the same way, your past mistakes have not reduced your value – they can**not**. Your present indiscretions cannot affect your value. Heartbreak is a really intense feeling of pain, yes, but your heart didn't actually break.

That guy or babe who hurt you did not "take a piece of your heart with them"; your heart is actually still intact.

God didn't shake His head and say, "You're so stupid; you should have seen the signs! Now you're crying? You deserve the pain."

God never says we deserve the pain. In fact, He wants to help us heal:

He heals the broken-hearted and binds up their wounds. (Psalm 147:3 NKJV)

There is no damage to your value in God's eyes just because you think you made a mistake. Mistakes hurt, yes, but they don't reduce our value. You don't stop looking like your parents just because you got drunk and did something stupid. Your DNA does not change just because you bashed the car.

Sometimes, where we get it wrong is that we try to fix ourselves up. We feel shame when we get hurt ("How could I have been so gullible? I'll never be stupid again.") And we feel shame when we make mistakes ("I shouldn't have done that. I will never let myself get carried away, again.")

It is in those "I'll never ___ again" sentences that we start to build walls, little by little, until we block love out completely.

From the moment my dad identified that I didn't know how to receive love, I've been on a journey to learn love, to allow myself to receive love, and learn to love myself so that I can eventually learn to give love, freely.

With each experience and failed relationship, I've been faced with the option to choose to build more walls or to break them down and risk letting love in.

At first, like most of us singles believe, I thought I was on a journey to learn how to receive romantic love. I thought the only hurt that would be uncovered would be from exes and almost-relationships; boy, was I wrong.

Everything in my life has been turned upside down and inside out: from childhood memories to seemingly silly disappointments from parents and siblings, to aspects of my character that I didn't know I needed to address. God has exposed weaknesses, tendencies and flaws. He has disciplined and corrected and broken down and re-moulded and reintroduced me to a version of myself I barely recognise.

It turns out that the walls I thought I had built to protect myself from romantic heartbreak actually had its foundations in the disappointments and hurt I experienced from other experiences, growing up – and everything had to go.

When I started sharing tips on How to be Single on my Instagram page, I thought I was doing a series that would teach people how to deal with pressure and cope with loneliness while waiting for romantic love. I thought that was the goal. I've since learnt that it is *not* the goal.

My single friends, we are not really looking for the love of others; we're looking for something deeper: our sense of value, our worth. We don't even know what it would look like or how to find it, but we are aware that it's missing. We don't even remember when we had it, but we are aware that we lost it somewhere along the journey of life.

I believe that Learning How To Be Single is the process of charting our path to recover our sense of value and love.

Where I Lost Myself

I'm not sure where I first lost myself, but sometimes I have flashbacks of things I used to say and do and I think, "Where did that girl go?"

I used to stand in front of the mirror and talk in different voices, making up characters and scenarios. I would come back from school, go straight to the mirror and have the best time just acting, I suppose is what it was. I'm not sure when it changed, but one day it became "stupid", so I stopped.

I used to sing in front of the fan. Then I would make speeches in front of an imaginary audience as I pretended to receive an award for my latest hit.

I acted out my documentaries – you know, those "Life of a Star" type ones where they would talk to the superstar's family members about the superstar (me), to find out what she was like as a child.

"She was always singing and acting and dancing all over the house," I answered, on behalf of my parents.

When my younger brother and I were the only ones at home, I terrorised him with my performances. When he complained, I said to him, "If I don't do this, what will you tell them when they ask you about my childhood? Now you can tell them how your sister wouldn't stop singing in your ear!"

I knew I didn't have a naturally wide range, so I practiced with Mariah Carey and Whitney Houston and Christina Aguilera – again, in my brother's ear.

But, one day, I stopped singing.

My other brothers were older and we weren't as close, so I didn't bother them with my singing. My dancing, though, everyone experienced. I would record music videos and play them over and over, learning the steps. I remember feeling so accomplished when I finally got the steps to Aaliyah's *More Than a Woman*, down.

But, one day, I stopped dancing.

I auditioned for a play in my final year of university – and I got the part! But I quit during rehearsals because I had schoolwork. And, one day, I stopped acting. I forgot I had ever wanted to act, altogether.

I remember when I realised that I would never be able to achieve the dreams I had held on to for my entire life. I was in my final year of university and Real Life loomed scarily ahead. I realised I hadn't been scouted by any talent agencies, hadn't started my amazing career, had no hopes of convincing my parents to let me go off to Hollywood to pursue a dream I had never even told them about and I felt a wave of panic coming over me. But I don't panic – that's for crazy, eccentric people and

I'm calm and logical and practical. So I quickly started to come up with a new plan, one that would allow me to remain creative, while also earning a respectable living.

I chose fashion; this was my plan: I was going to apply for a Masters in Fashion Management so that I would have transferrable management skills while I explored my creative side. I pitched this plan to my dad and he seemed to be on board with it – until he wasn't.

Never mind, then, I'll just find a way to do short fashion courses here and there. My dad agreed to pay for short courses to Central Saint Martin and I loved it, but I had to come back home and be practical.

I got a job as an associate producer on a makeover show, which was close to fashion but more sensible. Then I worked in an art foundation, which was still creative but not at all related to what I wanted to do.

And, what was it that I wanted to do, again – producing or fashion or something like that?

I had forgotten.

I became this person who did every single personality test, trying to remember who I was. I studied the horoscope for clues. I did the temperament quiz, the Myers Briggs quiz, even the "what Harry Potter character are you" quiz. I had always been interested in names and what they meant, but I became even more interested; what did my name signify? Was it "Omo *to* ayo" or "Omo *ti* ayo"? The more intellectual, "the child is worth joy" – as if my parents figured, "well, we didn't want this one but you know what, a child is a good

40

thing; we don't mind, after all." Or was it the more emotional, "the child we're happy to have"? Was I an intellectual conclusion or an emotional celebration? Did it even matter; was there really a difference?

Then there was the matter of my mind: I could be wildly creative and expressive, but also deeply logical and restrained. I could make myself answer yes to both sides of the "Are you Right-brained or Left-brained?" quiz. Was I both? Was one a cover-up for the other? Like, did my creative side only come out when I didn't want to do serious brainwork? Or did my logical side only come out to bully my creative side and keep her from embarrassing the family?

Maybe I'm the crazy one but if you've ever asked, "Why do you like me?" in a relationship – Like, the guy met you, liked you, asked you out, you said yes and now you're both happy, but then you become suspicious: "Does he *really* like me or is he just pretending? What about me does he like? Maybe he thinks I'm someone else, a picture he painted in his mind. Or the picture I painted for him. Maybe he'll find out who I truly am and change his mind and leave me" – If you've ever done this, then you kinda get what I'm saying. You ask these questions over and over again because you're not sure within yourself that you're valuable or worthy, so you're secretly hoping he'll say something nice so that you'll finally find something about yourself to like.

That's what I was doing with every aspect of my entire life.

My friends say I'm very analytical; I think it's because I'm still searching for clues to help me clarify who I'm really meant to be.

Do you remember the first time someone told you you couldn't dance, so you stopped dancing? And now you tell everyone, "I don't dance," like it's a badge of honour. Or the first time someone told you you couldn't make money off your dream, so you stopped dreaming... and told yourself you had "grown out" of your childish dreams. And yet, you follow all these people on social media who are successfully making a living out of the same childish dream?

We make up all kinds of practical-sounding excuses to validate our choices even though we are surrounded by examples of people who also had silly dreams – but followed them all the way through.

We lose ourselves over the journey of life, little by little, as uneventful as losing an earring or losing a sock. Bit by bit, people and circumstances steal the unshakable sense of wholeness that we are born with, until we become Practical Adults who have no idea what we're really doing. We simply wake up one day and realise, "I don't do that, anymore," and we never bother to ask why.

We don't understand how important those little things are in helping us paint the picture of who we are; how, with each piece lost, we lose a little bit of our courage and freedom to be who we were born to be: open-hearted, loving, generous, kind, optimistic.

We're not all meant to be actors and singers and dancers – or whatever else we dreamed of when we were children – but we are meant to be free to express ourselves without worrying that we don't deserve it, being afraid of disappointing people, or worrying that people would take advantage of us.

Finally Tired

I remember exactly what forced me to run to God.

I had met this guy, my exact spec. Tall, dark, intelligent, cool. Kind. Very sweet, very attentive. The sparks flew almost immediately. In two weeks, we had seen each other like, five times, not counting the actual day we met. We shared music, he told me stories, we danced, we stared into each other's eyes and smiled, held hands… all those mushy things.

Then it didn't work out. I was wildly attracted to him but I didn't want to have sex. I wanted to wait until we had fallen in love and got married to make the picture perfect. I wanted to be that special to him that he would want to wait.

He was polite about it. Told me he respected my decision – admired it, even – but he that wasn't what he wanted, and that was it.

I couldn't believe it. He still liked me, it was so clear. Whenever we were out together, he would sort of revolve around me. We still met up, hung out, talked – but he never tried to be physical with me again.

I hoped he would wake up one day and realise he cared about me too much to let what we had go. I thought about how happy I would be and how I would surprise him by letting him have it after all. I mean, it was just sex and I wanted to be with him. I just needed him to want to be with me without sex, first, you know?

It never happened.

I cried and cried. I was mad at myself for bringing up anything about sex.

One of my friends said to me, "Ah ahn, you could have just played the game until he was in too deep," and I agreed. It's not my first rodeo, as they say.

I was angry with God. Yeah, I brought Him into it. I begged Him to make it work out, to make my guy want me enough to just say yes.

I threatened Him, "This stupid sex thing is what's keeping me from being with this guy. It's not worth it!"

I cried, "Please, please. I want him so much. You can touch his heart, please."

Listen, this thing dragged for like a year. We would hang out, then not talk for a while, then he would call me and it would be all sweet and deep conversations, then he would drop me at home without even trying anything.

The guy eventually got married on my head.

I was so angry with God. I blamed Him for everything but I realised something: how could I, a "child of God", want something *so badly* that God very clearly *did not want* for me?

Let me give you a little context:

When I was in my first year of university, I was in the worst relationship. He wasn't physically violent at all, but just being in that relationship destroyed my sense of value. It was the most horrific experience of my life. He would call me, ask me to meet him outside my hostel and, if I wasn't there when he drove by, he wouldn't park or call me or wait. He would drive off.

Meanwhile, I would get there, say, five minutes after the call and wait, thinking he hadn't got there yet. Half an hour later I'd call, "*Ah ahn*, where are you?"

"You weren't there when I drove by so I drove off. I can't be waiting for you outside Moremi!"

After that, I started to run down when he called, just so I could make the drive-by.

That was just one of the very many reasons why I should never have been with him.

I remember praying then, too, knowing I shouldn't be in the relationship. But I really wanted it and God still allowed it – and I use the word, "allow" very loosely. What I mean is that I prayed but I still continued, because there was something to continue – the guy was still there. He treated me like crap but I allowed myself to be the crap and we continued like that.

In the case of this other guy, however, God prevented me from entering in completely. He didn't roll His eyes and say, "Let Me just allow it; she'll learn her lesson." It was as if He said, "There'll be no lesson to learn in this case. I forbid it."

In one case, I suffered, but at least I got what I wanted. In the other case, God said no: an undeniable, incontestable, no.

When I begged God to let me just be with this guy, I actually said, "Please let me be with him, even if I get hurt – but please don't let me get hurt too badly." But God didn't even allow that.

So I thought, how far away from God must I be, to desire something that He won't even allow? And, in the context of horrible things in the world – the plagues of Egypt, natural disasters, dictatorship, slavery – God appears to allow some pretty horrible things to happen. If He can figure out how to work those things together for good, but refuses to allow *this one thing*, I must have been so far away from God, I might as well have been walking on the path to hell.

Like, even with the power of my free will, God said no.

I thought it was impossible to get to the end of God's patience, but here I was, at the end of it. That scared me.

Yes, I was still angry with Him, but I prayed, "I can't do this anymore. If I can want someone so badly who You absolutely don't want for me, I must be getting something really wrong. I want to know Your heart, so that I'll know what pleases You, so that I'll never get it wrong, again. So, please, You choose. I don't want to choose for myself anymore. I only want who You choose for me."

I made a pact with God that my heart would be closed until He opened it, that I would not choose unless He chose first. I surrendered my dating life to God.

Feel free to borrow my prayer – then buckle up. This journey with God is wilder than a rollercoaster.

Surrendering

Surrendering is a tricky thing. As Christians, we think we can make arrangements with God and still get to make our plans.

I had never surrendered anything to God before, so I thought the act of me crying and begging was enough to prove that I was ready, and that He would send me a man, overnight. I didn't realise that what I had done was to surrender the desire I valued the most, which meant I had essentially invited God to come and *become* the desire I valued the most.

I didn't know that, but God did; the entire Father, Spirit and Son of the Trinity were ready for me.

At the time, I didn't have the courage to be a writer so I was working as a creative writing teacher, instead. I had also started a production company with three of my friends, but it wasn't making any money at the time and

I didn't feel like I was contributing any real value to the company. I felt like the other members of Destiny's Child that no one really cared about.

I hated being asked what I did for a living, but I learnt how to say, "Producer" when I wanted to be impressive, and "Teacher" when I wanted to be dismissive. And when people said, "That's so cool," all I could hear was condescension and it irritated me.

My parents thought the company was a joke. My dad didn't mind the idea of teaching; it was a respectable vocation for a woman. There wouldn't be a lot of money, but it would do. However my mum told me it was a waste of my talents. She didn't mean it in a hurtful way, only that she knew in her gut that it wasn't where I was supposed to be. She was right, of course, but I didn't know where I was supposed to be, either, and I didn't know who to turn to for help.

So, there I was, struggling with the need for love and not understanding my value, not knowing what I was supposed to be doing in life but wishing I would just "snap out of it" and find a sustainable way to make money – because if I figured that out, then it wouldn't be so bad that I was single. Like, being single and rich is fine; being married and poor-ish was alright. But being single and broke? That was a fail on all sides.

I ran into God the only way I knew how: I went to church every Sunday.

I really enjoyed listening to sermons, so I started listening to other sermons online. I signed up for a discipleship course at church and found a fellowship to go to every Monday. My life was surrounded by God.

I still loved going out dancing with my friends, but gradually noticed that listening to regular music made me long to have someone to hold. It goes back to being in secondary school, listening to slow songs on the radio and wishing there was someone I could dedicate the songs to. Or, when I was in uni and my friends and I would go dancing, certain songs would come up and we would go, "I need a guy to dance with!"

It was that feeling.

It's very inconvenient to feel that way when you've just surrendered your romantic life to God. The temptation to text someone and just hang out, all the while secretly hoping it would end up being more than that (and, maybe, just maybe, he would decide we could work it out. Maybe God will change him). Maybe, maybe, maybe.

I could listen to music anywhere – in the car, in my room, at a wedding, in a club – but I would get in my feels and spiral into a mood, cry, lash out at God and try to break the rules. It happened over and over until I made the connection that I only felt that way when I listened to regular music. Whenever I listened to sermons or Christian music, I didn't feel that way.

I had to give up my music.

I can't explain how painful this was. It was like giving up a part of myself; I had practically grown up with the radio; lying down next to the speakers with a book in my hand used to be my happy place and now I had to give it all up.

I still miss it, still wish I could listen to music for hours on end. And, whenever I try it, the same thing still happens – I still get mood swings and extreme feelings of loneliness that take hours of sermons and Christian music to erase.

For some people it's not music, it's movies, series, YouTube, novels or even social media.

For some of you, it's certain friends or family members; all it takes is one word to trigger something you thought you had overcome and you find yourself spiralling back to an old temptation or an old way of thinking.

It's not their fault – it's not the music's fault, or the friend's fault. You're the one who is trying to change something, not them.

If you have to cut yourself off from your triggers, don't blame anyone or anything, and don't expect anyone to go on the journey with you, too.

Your journey to valuing yourself is not a partnership.

Just do it. You're worth it.

The New Rules of Dating

Dating used to be simple: you dress up, look hot, go out, get hit on, someone asks for your number and you decide whether or not you want to give it, flirt a little, go home, google his name (search for him on Facebook, find your mutual friends and find about him) wait for the call, go on a few dates, explore your sexual compatibility and, if he wants commitment and you do, too, make it official.

But I was now a church girl. I was reading the bible and getting transformed from the inside, out. They say that once you surrender to God, everything changes and you meet the right person immediately. In fact, one of my closest friends and I had similar Single journeys. She had also surrendered and, next thing you know, she was dating this Tall, Dark, Handsome man of God. A few months later, she was engaged. I was excited! It was evidence that this surrendering thing works!

"*Ah ahn*, look at my homie getting married, just like that, God did it!"

And I was so ready for mine!

Years later I was still single. Time was passing and nothing was happening. Wasn't God happy with me, yet? Hadn't I surrendered enough?

Maybe my height preferences were restricting my options, I thought, so I lowered them. Then, did I really have to be physically attracted to him? Maybe attraction is just vanity, and a real godly church girl wouldn't care about that.

I wasn't ready to surrender that one.

Maybe that was why. Maybe God was waiting for me to surrender my desire to be attracted to my husband, then I'll find out that he had always been right in front of me, with his oversized trousers belted up to his waist, a short, fat tie resting atop his too-big short-sleeved shirt, Complete Jewish Bible in hand, waiting for the eyes of my understanding to be enlightened so that I would recognise him as the bone of my bone.

I was afraid that letting God choose meant that I would end up with someone I would have to shut my eyes, lie on my back and count to ten until it was over, with. The thought made me shudder, then repent of my sins and shudder again. Clearly, I wasn't surrendered enough.

And, since I was already there, I had a question for God: if we weren't allowed to factor in sexual desires on this surrendered dating journey, wouldn't dating a Church Boy be boring? I mean, what would you... do, together; read the bible and pray? Take long walks whilst making sure to avoid physical contact? Shake hands or side-hug? If you couldn't flirt or go dancing or cuddle, what was the difference between just being friends and being romantically interested?

I used to go to this really amazing fellowship that changed my life. We would talk about very real issues like, "Is it really possible to be in a romantic relationship and not have sex?" "Aren't church-boys really just boring?"

The guys would counter with, "See, good girls really want bad boys. This Church-boy thing really doesn't favour us."

As we grew in our relationship with God and, because we were able to be so open in our conversations, we eventually accepted that it was possible to be celibate. Then, new questions cropped up, "Is kissing allowed?" "Can you sleep over – even if you don't do anything?" "Can you sit on your boyfriend's laps?" "What if you don't have sex; how far can you explore?"

We eventually agreed that all forms of foreplay were dangerous, that it was difficult but possible to have godly courtships and that God was our strength on the journey.

On my part, as a new church girl, I spent my time looking out for the potential one. You know that thing that happens with single people, where you walk into a room and immediately start to assess who you think could be a potential, who you can manage, *sha*, if it came down to it, and who you prayed God would please not force you to end up with?

It's all well and good to be open to receiving love, but it becomes a problem when you find yourself constantly assessing every Single person around you by their marriageability status. I call this, "Singleness Disease".

Singleness Disease:

An old friend sent me a link, once. It was the story of a woman who had been single for a long time. As she complained to her girls, one asked, "But, what about – " Let's call him, Usman. "What about Usman?"

"Ugh," this lady replied, derisively, "I could never marry Usman even if he was the last man on earth."

"What's wrong with him?"

"He's always all over me; he's just too nice. I don't want a pushover."

Years later, our lady was still single and Usman got married.

"Oh, no," she cried to herself, "I really missed out on a good guy."

Hurt by the implication of my friend's message, I scoured through the list of guy friends I had. Who did she think my own Usman was? I knew there was no one around me who was vying for my affections but I started to doubt that certainty. I would look at every friend of mine, every friendly guy, every passing male figure and wonder, "Who am I overlooking?"

This is Singleness Disease: the fear of missing out on the right person, leading to second-guessing yourself, second-guessing your relationships and disrupting your peace. Listen, ladies, it is not your responsibility to try to make a guy want a relationship with you.

I have a few really close guy friends. We've been friends for a few years. We've seen each other through painful relationships, prayed together when we believed we'd found the one, cried together when it turned out they were, in fact, *not* the one, and continued to hold each other up through life, work, business and faith. But every time I hung out with any one of them in any public setting, I felt the pressure of the question, "Why can't it be him? What if it's him? You're already friends; you know they say the best relationships start off as friendships."

After years of being single and coming up with "10 steps to check if he could be The One", I had self-helped myself into a trap. While I wasn't romantically interested in my friends, I was always checking guys – all guys – against my rules and regulations. This meant that, whenever someone "passed" the minimum regulations test – loves God, has ambition, isn't ugly – a troubling question popped up, "Could it be him?"

It didn't matter that I wasn't attracted, interested or, most importantly, being courted, by said person, the question popped up in my head, regardless. People say that women "know how to get a man to choose her if she wants" and, even though my life is evidence that this isn't factual, I started to worry that it was my fault for not encouraging every guy around me to get on my case.

I'd be chatting with a friend when a voice would whisper, "Can't you see him? And you think you'll find someone else who would understand you. You're going to be single forever, at this rate."

Clearly, that's not the voice of God, but it still tormented me constantly. People around me and these friends of mine would smile suggestively or out rightly challenge me, "Omotayo, what's wrong with him? You're too picky."

Again, ladies, it is not your responsibility to try to make a guy want a relationship with you!

And, guys, you don't have to talk to every girl just to prove that there's nothing wrong with you, either.

Sometimes, the people who perpetuate Singleness Disease think they're doing it for the right reasons. "My intentions are good," they say, but they're just passing their fear along to you. *They* don't understand – or don't remember – what it's like to be single and hoping, they don't remember what it's like to wonder whether you're being too easy or too difficult. They don't remember the anxiety of waiting for someone to call and the disappointment when they don't.

They are afraid there's something wrong, "How can it be possible that there are no good guys? Or no good girls?" After all, they were once single, too, and now they're married; it must be your fault.

So they pass those fears on to us with the words, "What's wrong with him/her?" and "There's no such thing as a Perfect person," and they have no idea how much it messes with your own mind.

On the other hand, pressure only sticks when it finds agreement. It takes two to tango, as they say; no one can put you under pressure if you're not already under pressure, yourself. And if you're under pressure from within, it's probably because you believe that being in a relationship gives you value or proves that there's nothing wrong with you. Again, the answer isn't in a romantic relationship; it's in accepting your innate, intrinsic value.

Q: "But, if you shouldn't go around wondering who your husband is, how will you know?"

A: Any guy who is interested in you will say it.

The rest of this story serves as an example:

So, the guys at my fellowship were mostly alright. They all loved God, so I figured it meant that God approved of any of them. I mean, we're all believers, we'd all admitted to our desires and we all wanted to get married eventually, so I figured this was good ground to select from.

I allowed myself to develop a liking for one of them. He wasn't really my spec but I had repented of my desires so that was evidence that God would finally be pleased with me. And, yes, I know I said my heart was "closed until God opened it" but this was fellowship, so that was His go-ahead, right?

I mean, this guy was nice, he called to check up on me and he cared enough to pray with me when I needed someone to pray with. I had never had anyone take the reigns when it came to praying with me – beyond the quick, "have a safe trip in Jesus' name!" or, "I pray the meeting goes well!" –and I was impressed, so I stirred up affections toward him, started creating scenarios in my mind and, every time he called, I allowed myself to believe he was just warming himself up to declaring his intentions.

He never declared anything.

"Maybe this is how church guys are," I thought, "Maybe they just take their time."

It was on my birthday, about a month later, that I realised there must have been something wrong with my assessment.

I'd started the day hopeful for a special birthday call – if he could invite me to have ice cream on a normal day, my birthday would truly be special.

He never called.

I convinced myself to call him. "Maybe something happened. I don't just want to jump to conclusions."

I had already jumped to the conclusion that he liked me, why was I worried, now?

I called him, he picked up, said hello politely.

"How's your day?" he asked.

"Oh, it's going well. I don't really have any birthday plans."

"Oh, yeah, happy birthday."

Ouch.

"Thank you!"

And that was it.

My pride was bruised. I finally allowed myself to realise that the guy was just being nice because he was nice. He called to check up on me because he was trying to check up on me and he prayed for/with me because I needed someone to pray for/with.

The reason he didn't say anything about wanting a relationship with me was because he didn't want to be in a relationship me. Essentially, even though he was always there, he was romantically unavailable.

That was unusual for me, because I was used to guys being completely unavailable unless they wanted something. I started to see that these church guys could be fully emotional and open without being interested in dating you.

If you're making the transition from "worldly" dating to church life, it can be confusing.

Unfortunately, there are also many guys who know this and take advantage, manipulating the bond of "brotherhood" in the church to take advantage of our emotional vulnerability. At the same time, many of us ladies have painted romantic pictures in our heads as a result of Singleness Disease and found ourselves heartbroken.

It is important to be clear about the fact that not every friendly guy or prayer partner is someone you should date. It doesn't matter how many times you pray together, how many times he lets you lean on his shoulder when you're sad, how many words of prophecy he's had for you and how many you've had for him; it's not your responsibility as a woman to help him figure his feelings out.

If you really can't control yourself and absolutely have to ask, believe his answer! He may answer you indirectly, "I'm so flattered that you would even think of me that way… You're such an amazing person, any man would be lucky to have you as his rib." All that polite church-talk is his way of saying he's not interested.

"They all loved God, so I figured it meant that God approved of any of them."

I go into more detail about marriage and finding the One later in the book, but I'll quickly address this, here: there is an assumption that, as long as two people are Christians, their relationship can work, and/or God approves of it. This is deception and there is no truth in it!

There have been many heartbreaks between Christians; church attendance and even faith is not a sign that God wants you to be together.

Years ago, my cousin sent me a powerful teaching by Jon Courson about choosing a partner. He talked about the three parts that make up every human being: the body, the soul and the spirit.

The spirit is our true identity – the breath of God that gives us life and allows us to connect to God.

The soul is made up of our mind, imagination, thoughts, will, choices, decisions, feelings, emotions, preferences, tastes, and entire personality – all the things that make us distinct from each other.

The body is what allows us to express ourselves in the world through our sight, taste, touch, hearing, smell, speech.

According to the teaching, marriage is meant to be a relationship where two people connect on all three levels: body, soul and spirit.

A connection on one level alone is either a fling (body-to-body), a friendship (soul-to-soul) or a prayer-partner relationship (spirit-to-spirit); every marriage needs at least two out of three to work, but the most ideal combination for marriage is a complete three out of three.

I really like this theory as a general guide to identifying who a suitable partner would be, but I also believe that God likes to shake things up, sometimes. Some people aren't immediately attracted to each other; some people don't start off having the same spiritual beliefs, and some people develop similar interests over time.

The most perfect scenario would to find someone you can connect with on all levels – at a **time** when you are both ready for commitment. If you meet the perfect person at the wrong time, it still won't work. And since time is in God's hands, the entire thing is really up to Him.

In all of this, there is one universal rule: ladies, when a guy is romantically interested and ready to commit, he will let you know. You won't have to guess. If you have to guess, he doesn't want to commit.

There's no caveat to this. If he doesn't let you know and comes around months or years later, talking about how he used to like you, it means he didn't like you enough. And if he still doesn't tell you he's interested in a relationship, he may just be trying to see if he can manipulate your feelings to get something now without having to commit.

As a guy once said to me, men are visual. If you're around him, he has seen you. If he wants you, he will come to you. It doesn't matter whether you're in church or not.

Introducing Love

All my exes were moving on and getting married and I was still waiting on the Lord. Actually, I was waiting *for* the Lord. The difference is this:

You know when a couple just start dating and, let's say, it's the girl's birthday and the guy says to her, "I'm going to pamper you, this weekend. Whatever you want, I'm here for you."

She's hungry, he brings her food on a platter. She's hot, he fans her. She's tired, he massages her feet as she falls asleep on cushions he arranged, himself. He literally waits on her, hand and foot.

Waiting on God is like that; it is our love response to His love for us. He's so amazing and faithful in His Love toward us that we are eager to find every little opportunity to love on Him because it is so rare that there's anything we can do for Him.

Now, imagine a couple who have become tired of the demands of their relationship. They bicker and fight all the time – he never puts his plate in the sink. She takes too long to get ready, etc.

They rarely go out together but, one day, they have to go for a family event. Well, we've already mentioned that she takes her time getting ready so he has to wait.

He checks his watch every five minutes and sulks. He's waiting for her and she's wasting his time.

I believed God was wasting my time.

Did He know all the children I would have had by now? They would have been in secondary school if I had got married when I wanted. I would have snapped back fully, but now I'll have to deal with stretch marks and weight gain in my old age.

I still lived with my parents; didn't God know that was childish? I wanted to move into my marital home and start having the same problems my mates were having (in-laws, cost of diapers and school-fees) rather than still complaining about how my mum never throws anything away and there's clutter everywhere.

Oh, all the things I would have achieved for the Kingdom if only I was already married. Didn't God know I was going to work hard to have a marriage that would be the manifestation of Christ and the Church? All the submission I was diligently learning was wasting; no one to submit to. No one to respect, because we know that men only respond to respect. I had plans to wow my husband by kneeling for him, just to prove I wasn't too proud to do it. After all, Sarah called Abraham Lord and I was going to be blessed like her.

If only God would stop wasting my time.

My friend, Omilola, once shared something I found very profound. "When it comes to hearing God speak to us," she said, "we don't have a hearing problem; we have a love problem."

Her point was that we all hear God, but we don't all love God. Without love, we are impatient and frustrated and easily disappointed, so we are cynical and easily dismiss the many ways He tries to get our attention.

It has already been established that I had a love problem in life, so it's no surprise that I would have a love problem with God. But how was I supposed to correct that? How was I supposed to suddenly wake up one day and love God?

I was taking a discipleship course at church at the time and stumbled on a bible verse:

"By this all will know that you are My disciples, if you have love for one another." John 13:35 (NKJV)

The verse really ticked me off. I didn't believe it and I didn't agree with it.

"How can love be the identifying factor of a Christian?" I asked my class. "Ellen DeGeneres loves, and she's not a Christian. There are so many people who show love and are not Christians. How can Jesus Himself say that love is the singular thing that will identify and distinguish His Disciples on the earth?"

The problem with being a Christian, though, is that I claim to believe everything that is written in the bible.

So, how could I disagree with something Jesus said? It was right there, in colour red.

But how could I agree? Love wasn't a real thing, I thought, it was just an emotion people used to manipulate each other. When they were in love, they could make unfair demands on their loved ones under the cover of love, and when they weren't in love, they could break people's hearts and do stupid things under the guise of searching for love.

Even siblings didn't really love each other. They just lived in the same house until they were either old enough or rich enough to leave, make up their own families, and then they became those pesky extended family members who were always needing help or judging new wives or fighting for an inheritance or betraying your trust in one way or the other.

Parents – well, parents had to pretend to love their children because they were the ones who brought them into the world. But no one told them how tough it would be to raise good children so now, they were stuck with them and just had to do what they had to do in order to provide for their children. The love part was not an automatic part of the package.

I felt guilty for thinking this, seeing as I have parents and siblings, but I truly believed it.

So, here I was, wondering what Love was, and God had the answer.

The first thing He did was bring me a new friend, a guy I'd seen around who suddenly reached out to me. As a single girl, my first reaction was to block him off because I knew he was unavailable, but something in me told me to relax.

"Lord, You're clearly the One bringing him into my life, so You have to cover me," I said.

I knew it was God because my new friend immediately started talking to me about God.

"God is a Loving Father," he would always say.

Okay, but no one asked you, I would think.

"What is a Father?" He would ask. "Like, what is a Father like?"

"I don't know," I'd respond, confused. "I guess, strict but fair?"

Then he'd say, "Exactly. It's because you think Fathers are strict that you think God is strict."

And I'd be like, "Uhm, isn't God strict?"

"No, He's not."

"But if God isn't strict, then how about discipline and all that?"

"It's because we think of our Fathers disciplining us that we think God disciplines us."

"But the Bible says so!" I would protest.

Then he would switch to, "What is the Kingdom of God?"

Was this a trick question?

"Open your bible to Romans…"

Was this guy kidding?

"Look at it, what does it say?" I guess he wasn't kidding. "The Kingdom of God is Righteousness, Peace and Joy in the Holy Ghost."

"Okay?"

"That is the Kingdom. Righteousness, Peace and Joy."

I didn't understand what he was saying, but I could tell that he was trying to show me something about God's heart.

"God is a loving Father! A loving Father, not a strict Father."

Why was it important to make a distinction between those two things? Why couldn't God be strict *and* loving, at the same time?

About the same time all this was happening, I was on a Christian email thread where the conversation was on hearing from God. One of the guys on the thread said he had learnt to hear from God by asking Him to help pick out a tie to wear to work. Someone else agreed with him. The idea was, "ask God for the little things and work your way up to the big things."

"God doesn't care about what you're wearing!" I protested – but to myself, "He has more important things to focus on than to spend all His Heavenly energy on helping Usman choose between the striped tie and the dotted one."

Yet, the idea that the Almighty God could be interested in the silly little mundane details of our lives intrigued me. I decided to try it out for myself. What was the worst that could happen?

One day, I stood in front of my rack of clothes. Feeling really stupid and more than a little nervous, I said – on the off chance that God was listening – "Well. I'm just going to run my hand through the clothes and whichever one I stop on, that'll be the one You've chosen. Okay, God?" and I started to touch my clothes.

"This is silly," a voice in my head said, "What's going to happen, now? You'd better just pick something out yourself and stop expecting anything to happen."

But something did happen, my hand "felt" like stopping on a particular item. So I stopped, took it out and wore it.

"That wasn't so dramatic," I said to myself.

I continued to do that, day after day and, one day, it stopped feeling so silly.

Then I moved to makeup.

"This is stupid, Omotayo, there's absolutely no way God cares about what lipstick you're going to wear, today."

But, somehow, my hand stopped on one particular shade and I put it on.

Giggling with excitement, I started to "ask God" for makeup tips. I'd stand in front of my mirror and say, "I don't know what look to do, today. Please lead me to choose the right colours," then I'd pick up a brush and start.

Sometimes, I would pick up the same brush I "felt led" to use yesterday and feel like I should put it back down. Sometimes, I would choose a colour I wouldn't have chosen if I hadn't invited God to participate in the process. As time went on, I really started to believe that God *was* interested in my clothes, makeup and, eventually, even my hair and skin, then my room and chores, my driving, what I ate or didn't eat, how much time I spent on the phone, and on and on!

As I went on this secret little journey with God, I started to feel like He was my Friend. Not just a "strict Father" who is too busy with Important Things, but a friend who was interested in the little things that made up my day to day life.

If God could be interested in my lipstick, then it meant He could be interested in my gist. It meant we could talk about anything – not just when I was praying deep, serious prayers about Purpose and marriage – but even when I bumped my toe or felt like going to see a movie or had a silly fight with my friend or read a book I liked or anything at all!

That's when I started to understand why it was so important to make the distinction between seeing God as a Loving Father, versus seeing God as a Strict Father.

Character and Singleness

Chatting with God like He was my Best Friend was one thing, but figuring out what I was meant to be doing with my life was another. I was still single, still pining over exes, my mum was still asking questions about the ex who was engaged, I didn't know if I was in the right job, I felt broke all the time, and I had taken to wondering if I had made a mistake somewhere in my childhood and was reaping the consequences of, I don't know, dating that horrible guy in university or wanting to follow the creative path instead of a more structured path.

I had studied English for my first degree – by choice, not because I missed the cut off for Law! – and I'd done a Masters in Writing at the University of Warwick to legitimise my local first degree with a foreign one.

There was the production company but I've already touched on my severe impostor syndrome and so I had taken a teaching job in a primary school.

Teaching was tough. It was emotional and intense, like having to make a speech to three different audiences with different attention levels every single day, then having to mark and assess their writing in enough detail to help them improve, but not too much detail to confuse them (I failed at this!) And all the while, I had to be aware of their emotional needs, their personal struggles, their very different learning styles and the impact I was having on their lives.

I was all too aware of how some of my teachers had helped me believe in myself, growing up, while other teachers had dented my confidence, so I was always trying to be fair, not show favouritism, involve as many pupils as possible in the thirty minute timeslot, whilst making sure they understood the topic. Listen, teachers are superheroes.

As I watched the children, I saw how they put on different personas depending on who was talking and what was required of them. For instance, because I spoke a certain way, the pupils I taught tended to be as proper and articulate as they could be, when answering my questions. But when they were around the nannies and cleaners, they mimicked their informal way of speaking. I learnt that some of the children whose parents were away a lot were attention seekers and, sometimes, troublemakers, while the ones whose parents were attentive couldn't get away with being naughty.

I saw that children of troublesome parents were troublesome, and children of kind parents were kind. It went without saying that the children who knew how to fake tears and manipulate their teachers also picked it up from somewhere.

It was so easy to see when a child was neglected, and so difficult to handle it without crossing the silent teacher boundaries and upsetting the parents. It was tough to read the essays they wrote and not want to get involved, but it was impossible to do so without disrupting the peace of the organisation.

I realised that teachers who have taught for years have had to become like doctors: get over the sight of blood, don't get too attached to your patients, do the best you can in the time you have and keep it moving swiftly on.

I was new to the whole thing, so everything was super-deep to me. As I taught the children and made friends with some of them, I realised that children will become mirrors of who their parents really are when no one is watching, and not what parents appear to be in the larger society's opinion.

You can't hide your true character from your children; they imitate both your weaknesses and your strengths. They know when you're pretending to be okay and they learn how to pretend to be okay, too. They know when you're lying and they learn to lie, too. Yes, children also learn from their friends and teachers and TV, but the most powerful influence on a child's life is their parents.

Prior to this, I'd believed my flaws were "just how I was" and that I couldn't change. I did not like confrontation, I kept malice, internalised my pain and lashed out with sarcasm and cynicism. However, as I watched children be sarcastic, mean to their friends, form cliques and cut each other off, I realised that they had picked it up from other people who also didn't realise that they had a responsibility to be better because of how much they were influencing their children.

If I didn't learn to overcome these things in myself, I would only end up teaching my children how to have the same flaws. And, even worse, if I didn't learn how to correct myself, I would never be able to teach my children how to do the right thing.

I realised that I had made big plans to be a good girlfriend and wife and mother, but my fantasies of perfection were made up of the external things that people admired, and not the hidden flaws that only the closest family and friends could see.

That was when I decided to take my character seriously and it became my priority. Even as I hoped for love and marriage, I realised that there was a lot of work I needed to do on myself, first.

Teaching led me to my first lesson in making a good marriage: your character comes first. You can be with the nicest person in the world, but if you have character flaws that you're not willing to admit to and address, you will ruin it.

There's no point whining and saying, "If he loves me, he'll love me for who I am!" If who you are is mean, spiteful, unforgiving – and unwilling to change, you shouldn't be in a relationship with anybody.

No one is perfect, but anyone can be the right one if they are willing to work on their flaws. Anyone who refuses to acknowledge that they have issues that need to be dealt with will destroy every relationship they're in. They won't be able to keep friends, family members will keep them at arms length and they'll keep thinking everyone else is to blame for their isolation.

Refusing to apologise for hurting people's feelings and feeling entitled to remain mean is not "owning your truth", it's choosing to be flawed rather than owning up to the fact that there's something wrong, there.

I used to think it was cool to be really cold hearted and aloof. I could choose to be nice to whoever I wanted and I could shut out whoever I didn't like. Mess with me and I'll cut you with my words. Think I'm a snob? You're just mad because I don't like you – that was me. However, whenever I was in a relationship I was sweet and open. I liked the fact that dating allowed me to put my guard down; I felt like I could rest from my perpetual defensiveness when I was with someone who cared about me and I valued that, but then I started studying marriage and realised that there's so much more to a happy marriage than just falling in love.

I heard something interesting about marriage, once. The guy said, "In the different seasons in marriage, you'll end up treating your spouse however you treat the people around you. If you're rude to your help, a time will come when you'll be rude to your spouse. If you're condescending to your staff, a time will come when you'll be condescending to your spouse. If you don't communicate well with your parents, a time will come when you won't communicate well with your spouse."

The idea is that, beyond the romance you share with your spouse, you'll eventually show them every other side of you as you share your lives.

This meant that I couldn't just be nice to the guy I liked, I also had to be nice to the annoying driver, angry boss, stuck-up colleague, rude receptionist, all of them. I had to be in control of my personality and work hard to make sure I treated everyone with kindness and respect, so that I would always treat my spouse with kindness and respect – and be a good example to my children.

I told myself, "To be a good spouse, you have to be a good person all round; you can't pick and choose when to be kind."

Marriage was my goal and I wanted to make sure I scored.

Slowly – sometimes painfully – I became more patient, more considerate, more open and more positive. I didn't get married but I was a lot more content in myself. Quite frankly, it was the perfect setup to get me to fix up!

Studying Marriage

In my mind, marriage was the only platform that offered the potential of total acceptance, lifetime companionship, sexual pleasure, offspring and possibly financial stability. However, there was also the fear of being maltreated in marriage, being cheated on, being betrayed, not being able to sustain love, and the fear of being lonely even in the marriage relationship. Divorce has become commonplace and it adds to the fear and uncertainty, like, why go through the process of getting married at all, if there are no guarantees that it'll work out?

On my journey, I had many questions and many fears. One of my biggest fears was falling out of love with, or resenting my partner.

What if I go into the marriage thinking he's great, but end up resenting him for anything – from not supporting my dreams to being more successful than me? What if I need to keep relying on him for financial support; what would that do to my sense of my own value? What if he goes out and starts telling his friends that I don't contribute any value, simply because he doesn't recognise the value of being a wife and mother? What if he snubs my creative desires and thinks my goals are just indulgent hobbies? What if he withdraws from me and I'm stuck with him because I'm not financially independent enough to take care of myself and my children without him?

Outside of the marriage itself, I had more questions:

What is Submission, and why should women submit?

What is this whole "Love vs. Respect" thing, what if women want to be respected as well?

Is a marriage really about just the two people in it?

Can you marry anybody, as long as you decide to get married?

Do all men cheat in marriage?

Will your in-laws disrespect you?

How important is money?

How do you resolve conflicts?

Were our parents really happy in their marriages or did they just endure for the sake of culture and peace?

Is sex overrated?

If marriage is just about children and you can have children outside marriage, is marriage still important?

What does a Happy Marriage look like?

Does emotional abuse even matter?

Is divorce an unforgivable sin?

Do all men cheat?

How come men never trust their wives with their money?

What happened with Adam and Eve; whose fault was it in the Garden?

Why is God so interested in marriage?

Is marriage for everyone?

Why do we feel loneliness and sexual desires when we're single, if we're not meant to have sex until we're married?

Is sex before marriage really a sin; what if you're going to get married?

What if you get married and your spouse doesn't satisfy your sexual desires?

What if you get fat during/after pregnancy and your husband stops wanting you?

When considering marriage, is love enough? Should you marry for logic or for love?

If you marry a guy whose friends cheat, does it mean he'll cheat, too?

How involved should parents and extended family members be?

When children come, do couples stop loving each other romantically?

When is it okay to leave a marriage?

Is there such a thing as a "Soul Mate" or "The One"?
How do you find "The One"?

Can God tell you who your spouse is?

What if you don't want to get married at all? And on and on and on.

Prior to this season, where I admitted that I wanted to be married, the most research I had done about the institution was from movies – and bad relationships.

I don't remember who it was who said, "If you want to buy a car, you'll study the mileage, history, usage, purpose, function, design, cost and much more, before buying it. Yet, you want to choose a life partner without doing any real research about marriage."

I had a lot of questions, yes, but I didn't really try to find the answers; I just brushed the thoughts away and figured that it would work itself out, somehow.

After I started my journey, however, I started to look for answers.

Why do you want what you want?

One of the significant points of clarity for me started with the questions: Why did I want to be married? What had shaped my ideas of marriage, and where did my desires come from?

Sometime in 2013, the topic of marriage and relationships came up on my Christian email thread. The first question the admin asked was, "What are the three most important things you want in your partner?" The answers came flooding in. Of course, because we were Christians, everyone had some version of "God-fearing" on their list, but they also had other things; values, character, conflict resolution, family and background, etc.

Then the admin switched the question: "what three things do you have to offer that person?" The answers were immediately more reflective as we realised that we had high standards of other people, but lower standards of ourselves.

The question that really dug deep for me, however, was when an admin asked, "Why do you want what you want?" Basically, where did your desires come from?

Like, why do you want a tall guy? Is it because the last short guy you dated broke your heart?

Why do you want a generous partner? Is it because your parents weren't generous and you don't want to end up like them?

Why do you want a rich spouse? Is it because you're afraid of financial insecurity and you want to be able to rely on them?

Why do you want a sexy wife? Is it because you couldn't get the hot girls to talk to you when you were younger and now, you want to prove that you can do it?

Why don't you want to marry from a different tribe? Did someone around you have a bad experience?

In isolation, these are valid desires to have. But upon deeper reflection, I started to see that I had created a picture of an ideal life based on hurt and brokenness from our pasts. I wanted to be married because I believed it would be a safe haven and nothing bad would happen to me while I was in it because I would have someone to love me and cover me.

Again, there's nothing intrinsically wrong with that idea – except for the fact that it put a lot of pressure on someone else to "save" me.

God started with my external desires.

At first, I was frightened. While my list had values and character on it, somewhere, it also had "tall, hot, sexy" as well. So, of course, if God was going to "deal with" my desires, it meant He was going to give me the opposite of what I asked for, just to teach me a lesson.

That mindset is problematic because it makes God seem reactive and punitive. God is not going to "teach you a lesson" with the person you're going to spend the rest of your life with. He's not going to make your marriage a perpetual Naughty Corner.

I remember sharing my fear with one of my friends and she tried to help me see that God wasn't going to punish me for wanting to be attracted to my husband.

I said, "Well, maybe it's a matter of perspective. Like, if chocolate is bad for your health and God wants you to eat salads and healthy food, it'll feel like punishment because you're not used to it. But, really, it's for your own good."

Vehemently, she rejected that logic. "God doesn't have to choose between what tastes nice and what is good for you. He can give you someone who is both broccoli and chocolate."

And the church said, amen!

If we're "Complete in Ourselves", what is Marriage for?

Let's start from the very beginning.

In the garden of Eden, God made a bunch of stuff on the earth and He gave them the ability to procreate after their own kind – dog gives birth to another dog, orange tree "gives birth to" oranges, etc. But when He made human beings, He made them after *His* own image and likeness. So, in a way, God gave birth to human beings.

In this way, He showed us that when it comes to procreating and multiplying, we give birth to what we have inside of us. Everything animal and plant had the ability to reproduce and multiply from within it, which shows us that we don't need anything external to grow and increase (be fruitful, multiply, prosper).

Everything we need is inside of us – even love.

Adam was alone, but he had his love inside himself; he just needed God's help to bring her out.

"… The Lord God said, "*It is* not good that man should be alone; I will make him a helper comparable to him." Out of the ground the Lord God formed every beast of the field and every bird of the air, and brought *them* to Adam to see what he would call them. And whatever Adam called each living creature, that *was* its name. So Adam gave names to all cattle, to the birds of the air, and to every beast of the field. But for Adam there was not found a helper comparable to him.

And the Lord God caused a deep sleep to fall on Adam, and he slept; and He took one of his ribs, and closed up the flesh in its place. Then the rib which the Lord God had taken from man He made into a woman, and He brought her to the man.

And Adam said, "This *is* now bone of my bones and flesh of my flesh; She shall be called Woman, because she was taken out of Man."

Therefore a man shall leave his father and mother and be joined to his wife, and they shall become one flesh.

And they were both naked, the man and his wife, and were not ashamed." (Genesis 2:18-25 NLT)

The animals had their own counterparts with which to be fruitful and multiply. Trees have seeds and are able to multiply themselves. So, the difference with Human Beings seems to be that God was the One who took on the responsibility of forming Eve for Adam: God chose her and made her for him.

Why didn't God just make another woman out of the ground? I believe He was using them as a picture of the unity that the Godhead shares. You see, one of the

89

biggest mysteries about God is the mystery of the Trinity. How are there three people in One? Is it even possible?

I have a theory. Please note that I am not a theologian, just a child of God who loves to engage her imagination with God, but I believe my theory can serve as a guide.

I believe that God uses creation to give us pictures, illustrations and analogies of how the Spirit works. For instance, the Bible compares Jesus to a Lion when talking about His Strength, and calls Him a Lamb, when talking about His Sacrifice.

I believe that when God said He was making Human Beings in His Image and Likeness, He was giving us a physical illustration of what He looks like.

From the first time the Human Being was created, there was a plan for a male and a female – Eve was not an afterthought:

So God created man in His own image; in the image of God He created him; male and female He created them. (Genesis 1:27 NKJV)

However, it wasn't until later that He revealed the hidden Female to the visible Male – it wasn't until the appointed time.

This is similar to how God is portrayed in the Bible. We see the Masculine Expression of God throughout the Old Testament until the New Testament, where Jesus speaks of the Holy Spirit coming as a "Helper". The Word "Helper" that is used to describe Holy Spirit is the same word that's used to describe the Woman as a "Helper Comparable to Him" or "Helpmeet" in Genesis. Many theologians believe that Holy Spirit portrays the Feminine Expression of the Godhead – the Helper, Comforter, and Nurturer; very similar to how Mothers are portrayed.

Jesus, the Son, completes the Trinity, the same way children complete families. Each child then "leaves father and mother" to create their own family.

When we look at Adam and Eve, and even their children, we see that they all came out of One Source. Eve came out of Adam, their children came out of Eve. And, so, isn't it clear that they were always one, from the beginning?

I believe that the idea of Marriage – and, by extension, family – is a human illustration of the way God operates: His Oneness and His Triune expression.

"A man leaves his father and mother and is joined to his wife, and the two are united into one." This is a great mystery, but it is an illustration of the way Christ and the church are one. (Ephesians 5:31-32 NLT)

So, if we're "Complete in Ourselves", what is Marriage for?

Because we are made from God to look like Him (His Image) and be like Him (His Likeness), we are also made to express God's personality, character, purposes and plans. Marriage allows two complete individuals to express a different side of a complex and multifaceted God in a unique way.

And, because God's nature is vastly more multifaceted than we can imagine, it also means that every marriage can be unique and different – because God may want to show something new and different about Himself.

Two different marriages can follow different "rules" and still be truly united in Love, because they are templates that express different sides of God.

Finding "The One"

Obviously, in this day and age, God no longer uses physical ribs to create spouses, but I think we can still borrow some guidelines from the Bible passage in Genesis to get a general idea:

"... The Lord God said, "*It is* not good that man should be alone; I will make him a helper comparable to him." Out of the ground the Lord God formed every beast of the field and every bird of the air, and brought *them* to Adam to see what he would call them. And whatever Adam called each living creature, that *was* its name. So Adam gave names to all cattle, to the birds of the air, and to every beast of the field. But for Adam there was not found a helper comparable to him.

And the Lord God caused a deep sleep to fall on Adam, and he slept; and He took one of his ribs, and closed up the flesh in its place. Then the rib which the Lord God had taken from man He made into a woman, and He brought her to the man.

And Adam said, "This *is* now bone of my bones and flesh of my flesh; She shall be called Woman, because she was taken out of Man."

Therefore a man shall leave his father and mother and be joined to his wife, and they shall become one flesh.

And they were both naked, the man and his wife, and were not ashamed." (Genesis 2:18-25 NLT)

1. The Lord God *Said.*

If Marriage is an illustration of God, then only God can decide that it is time for anyone to be married. He's the One who knows *what* aspect of His nature He's trying to illustrate with our lives, so He's the only One who can say, "Okay, it's time."

2. I Will Make Him A Helper Comparable to Him.

After God has decided that it is time, after God has identified what aspect of His divine nature He's trying to illustrate through a marriage, then He chooses a partner that fits that particular nature or illustration.

Let's use the Colour Wheel as an illustration of this: Every colour can be mixed with another colour to create a third colour. However, when an artist is painting, he doesn't say, "all colours are good; let me just choose any combination." No, he thinks about what he's painting, then figures out what colour is best to depict it, then mixes the right colours to create the perfect shade.

If he's trying to paint green grass, he'll mix yellow and blue in the right proportion to create the exact shade of green he needs to depict the grass in the best way.

Someone may not be the right fit for you but be the perfect fit for someone else. That's because God is trying to create a different "colour" out of them.

Remember, the same way every colour is whole and complete on its own, you are complete on your own. Marriage creates a unique shade out of the combination of two complete "colours."

Trying to change your colour to match just anyone is unfair to both you and the other person. No matter how different or weird you may think your "colour" is, there's a perfectly complementary shade for you on God's colour wheel.

3. "... To see what he would call them."

A Name is an identifier. It carries the attributes and characteristics of a person, animal, place or thing – like a Noun.

When God has determined that it is time for marriage and has decided what He wants to illustrate, God does something interesting: He starts to involve the individuals on the journey.

He gave Adam a task.

When parents or teachers give children tasks, those tasks are meant to teach and train the children. And one of the first things children need to learn is how to identify things: objects, colours, shapes, people.

The teacher points to a dog and asks, "What is this?"

The child answers, "Dog!"

"That's right," the teacher says. "And what is the difference between you and a dog?"

"The dog walks on its hands, but we eat with our hands. The dog barks but we can talk!"

And on, and on.

In the early days, the children make mistakes, here and there. But as they continue going to school, they learn to correctly identify things.

God gave Adam the same homework, teaching him daily in His Presence by His Spirit until Adam learnt how to **correctly identify** the things in the Garden.

If Adam hadn't learnt how to identify the objects in the garden, he wouldn't have recognised the woman, his counterpart, when God brought her to him.

4. A Deep Sleep

Have you ever lost something – your glasses, your phone, your keys – and spent hours and hours searching everywhere for it, without any luck? And then, just when you had given up – maybe you decided to go and sleep – you woke up, groggily walked to the bathroom and found it right there?

This is the illustration that comes to mind when I think of a "deep sleep"; that state of mind where you've finally stopped trying to do and work and prove, and you finally decide to rest in God.

One of my friends shared her experience of meeting her husband. She had dated all kinds of guys and had her heart broken over and over again, but when she finally surrendered and said, "God, I give up! I'm tired of the cycles of heartbreak!" She met him.

There's something about truly resting – not pretending to rest, like I've done for years – that brings clarity and direction.

It was when Adam was truly at rest in God that God went to work on Eve.

5. The Rib.

Why did God choose the Rib? I have yet another theory – my previous disclaimer is valid here, as well.

We've established that Adam – the Male expression – was the external image that could be seen before God brought the Woman out. So, he's like an outer covering, which represents external protection and external provision, taking care of external, physical needs.

In contrast, God crafted the Woman from a Rib that came from the inside and couldn't be properly seen from the outside.

Ribs typically function to cover and protect internal organs – the heart, lungs and stomach. They give structure and form and are made from bones – a superhard substance. Ribs have shielding functions and protect the body against impact. They also have connecting and carrying functions: blood vessels and muscle tissue "hang" on the ribs and they help hold the organs in place. Ribs shield the sensitive internal organs and carry connective tissue.

This paints a picture of mutual covering: the flesh provides a covering for the bones, and the bones – the Rib, specifically – provides a covering for the heart and lungs, with partial protection for the intestines, spleen, kidneys, liver.

External flesh is active and protective. Ribs carry, connect and protect – this is the picture of the partnership in marriage.

6. He Made The Rib Into a Woman.

Every woman is born with everything she needs for life – and everything she needs to be the equal counterpart of a man in a Godly marriage, should she desire it. But, much the same way Adam needed to learn how to name the animals and tend the garden, the woman has to learn how to be a "rib": to help, protect, nurture, connect.

And, the same way it was God who taught Adam, it was only God who could mould Eve.

If God had presented Eve to Adam in the raw form of physical bones, he would only have seen her hard exterior. God fashioned her into her feminine expression and equipped her to play her part, then gave her a similar appearance to the man so that he would recognise her.

Every woman has the raw strength to thrive, dominate the earth and conquer territories. Every woman who God desires to place in a marriage must also allow herself to learn how to harness that strength in the context of a mutual partnership. She must recognise her value and live confidently in her identity. She must also understand that her male counterpart also has immense value and strength and learn how to harness her strength in a way that matches his, to express the nature of God that the marriage represents.

7. He Brought Her To The Man

After God had formed the rib (raw strength and potential) into a Woman (feminine expression), He brought her to the man.

Remember, Adam was in a deep sleep. He wasn't restless, and he definitely wasn't hunting. He was resting.

At the same time, the Woman wasn't stressed out. She had waited patiently, tucked away in her hidden place inside him until God brought her out. And, even after God brought her out, she didn't run around trying to draw the man's attention – we have already established that Adam wouldn't even have been able to recognise her in her raw form as a rib.

She waited for God to do His Work in her – softening her hard edges, shaping her curves, programming her like a computer software to execute His Divine Purpose.

And when God was done, He led her to the place where the Man was. It was God who woke the Man up. It was God who made the introduction.

It is God who leads us to His place of divine positioning; we can not position ourselves without His Leading. When a man is in the place God has chosen for him, God will bring his wife to him.

When a woman allows herself to be taught and led by God, God will bring her to her husband.

8. And Adam *Said*.

Commitment must always be sealed with our Words of agreement. The bible says that it is with our heart that we believe, but it is with our mouths that we confess. It is important that we say what we know God has placed in our hearts, or the process remains incomplete.

The bible tells us that even the demons believe that Jesus is the Son of God (James 2:19). Yet, it also tells us that those evil spirits will never confess that Jesus is Lord (1 John 4:2-3).

Isn't this interesting? It shows us that we can know or believe anything, but it is only when we confirm that belief with our words that we prove that we *agree* with what we believe; and it is only then that the Word has permission to become real.

Adam didn't just see her and know in his heart that she was the one; he said it out loud to her, with God and all of creation as his witness.

The witnesses are important: even God had witnesses (the Spirit and the Word) when He was creating the World.

9. They Were Both Naked, And Were Not Ashamed.

This is the evidence of Godly compatibility: the freedom to be yourself with another person without shame. But let me qualify this definition of "Freedom":

The Bible says that we will know where the Spirit of the Lord is, because there will be Freedom.

In a Godly marriage, both man and wife will honour and value each other's authentic personalities. You won't need to pretend to be less than you are, or to fulfil expectations that God never expected of you. There will be no need to hide and keep secrets for fear of being judged or rejected.

And even where we have weaknesses, we will be confident that our counterpart will cover us lovingly, while helping us correct them – and the blueprint will always be God.

Marriage is a union of two people who God has trained, taught and built up – and if you've ever seen a military training site, you know that training is a tough process. With God, it's even tougher, because He doesn't only work on our bodies, but on our minds, relationships, character, strengths – our entire spirit, soul and body. The process continues in marriage, so we can expect marriage to have its bumps and bruises, but because God is our guide, our help and our foundation, we also know it will be beautiful.

For we are His workmanship, created in Christ Jesus for good works, which God prepared beforehand that we should walk in them (Ephesians 2:10 NKJV)

Marriage Q&A

The previous study of the proper origin and purpose of marriage should clear up the millions of doubts we have about it; still, let's use the information we have just received to respond to some of them:

What is Submission, and why should women submit?

When we understand that every Marriage is a reflection of God's nature, we can look at God for the answer to this.

While Jesus was on the earth, He constantly said that He did not do anything because He wanted to – He only allowed Himself to say what the Father was saying, and to do what the Father was doing (John 5:19). Jesus submitted to the Father.

And when the Bible speaks of the Holy Spirit, it says that Holy Spirit will not speak of His own accord; Holy Spirit will only Speak that which He has heard (from God), and Holy Spirit will never point us to Himself; Holy Spirit will only ever point us to Jesus (John 16:13).

Even the Father submits. The Bible says that the Father gave all authority in Heaven and on earth to the Son (Matthew 28:18).

Submission is the nature of God. We were made in His image and likeness, that is why we submit.

For the second half of the question "What about the men?" The Bible actually asks us to submit to one another:

Submit to one another out of reverence for Christ. (Ephesians 5:21 NIV)

However, I think the emphasis is on women to submit because we are an illustration of the feminine expression of God, which, using the analogy of the Rib, is the inner part of the body.

The rib cannot function safely or properly if it doesn't allow itself to remain inside – or under – the protective covering of the outer body.

What are the roles of both genders in Marriage?:

I looked up the origin of the word "Woman" and saw that it means "Wife". I looked up the origin of the word, "Wife" and saw that it means, "Woman". It is the same with the words, "Man" and "Husband".

It seems as if God always created the Man to act in his role as a Husband, and the Woman to act in her role as a Wife.

The Bible defines gender roles clearly, even though it is obviously tainted with the limitation of cultural translations and patriarchal re-interpretation. Even beyond that, however, there's a simple way God sees all

Human Beings: in relation to our spiritual identity as Children of God we are both Son and Bride.

That is to say, both men and women are Sons of God, and both men and women are the Bride of Christ.

In our identity as Sons of God, we have the authority to be fruitful and multiply and take dominion over every territory. God blessed both Adam and Eve with this mandate when they were united and "gender-less" in Genesis:

So God created man in His *own* image; in the image of God He created him; male and female He created them. Then God blessed them, and God said to them, "Be fruitful and multiply; fill the earth and subdue it; have dominion over the fish of the sea, over the birds of the air, and over every living thing that moves on the earth." (Genesis 1:27-28 NKJV)

In our identity as the Bride of Christ, we are all the Body of Christ (the same way Eve was made out of the body of Adam). This speaks to our partnership with Jesus, seeing Him as the Head of the church, the same way wives are asked to see the husband as the head of the marriage.

For the husband is head of the wife, as also Christ is head of the church; and He is the Saviour of the body. (Ephesians 5:23 NKJV)

105

Our identity as Sons enables us to live on earth, to carry out God's assignment, and our identity as Bride enables us to become one with Christ.

In God's perspective, an unmarried woman is still a Bride and an unmarried man is still a Husband – he has a purpose that he must "leave father and mother" to actively fulfil, the same way Jesus did.

So, no, not everyone will get married; but everyone who believes in Jesus also believes that they will be reunited in marriage to Jesus at the marriage supper of the Lamb.

Must you marry a Christian?

There are many couples who weren't Christians when they got married, and went on to give their lives to Christ in the middle of it. There are others who were church-goers, who became more devoted along the way. There are also many who started off as believers and turned away from the path – whether for a season or completely.

My personal belief is that God is not limited in His ability to create a marriage that is a reflection of His nature. Let's take the popular example of Hosea, who was instructed to marry a prostitute. The purpose of his marriage and his children was to serve as a picture of God's frustration with the people of Israel, at the time.

We don't always start off knowing God's specific purpose for every specific marriage, but He will accomplish His goal.

Is sex overrated?

The desire for sex is strong enough that Paul, in the bible, encouraged people to get married if they couldn't restrain themselves. This suggests that sex is a powerful bonding act that deeply connects people who engage in it. As the most vulnerable act of intimacy and pleasure between couples, it is supposed to be like a special prize that you can only get when you're married, because it provides a safe space for you to be completely vulnerable with someone who has committed to love you, flaws and all.

Life is tough; as adults, we have to slug it out everyday in the marketplace – making ends meet, navigating career and work politics, managing relationships, serving others... it can be a lot to deal with. This is one of the primary reasons why people want to be in romantic relationships; we want someone to share life with, who also stirs up positive, comforting feelings in us, to share the burden and ease the stress that can be very mentally and emotionally demanding. Sex is a huge part of those "comforting feelings". Because it requires both parties to intentionally engage in giving the other pleasure, it creates a feeling of worthiness, gratitude, joy connection, love.

Sex is the sweet reward that couples can always look forward to in the middle of this tough life and it costs only love, nothing more.

When we have sex outside marriage, we are so connected and bonded, physically, that we end up overlooking the more important signs: do you have the same values? What is their character? Should you even be in a relationship with them? Sex goes from being this beautiful bonding act to a mask that blinds us from making the right decisions.

How many times have you heard someone say, "He or she is so mean but I keep finding myself going back"? Most of the time, it's the sex that keeps them there.

So, sex is not overrated. It is a crucial ingredient for the marriage bond. However, one of the reasons why people no longer believe that marriage is important is that they allow themselves to enjoy sex outside of it. I believe that sex makes marriage easier, but it makes it harder to make the right decisions when dating.

How do we deal with lust and sexual desires when we're single?

On its own, there's absolutely nothing wrong with feeling sexual desire when single; it's the same way there's nothing wrong with wanting to eat chocolate cake when you're on a diet, or wanting a new car when you can't afford it.

The difference between the person who wants a new car badly and saves up for it until they can afford it, and the person who wants a new car so badly that they break the law to get it is lust – lack of control.

In its simplest definition, lust is what we feel when we are overpowered by our desires. If your desire doesn't overpower your self-control, it's not lust.

For all that *is* in the world—the lust of the flesh, the lust of the eyes, and the pride of life—is not of the Father but is of the world. (1 John 2:16 NKJV)

The NLT version uses the word "Craving" in place of "Lust", and the Cambridge English Dictionary defines "craving" as "a strong or uncontrollable desire".

Anything you can't control becomes a beast and controls you. Like any other addiction, it becomes your biggest motivator and pushes you to justify doing things you know is wrong.

The first thing that helped me manage sexual desire was an understanding of the consequences. And, no, not pregnancy or disease – there are ways around those. The biggest consequence for me was another devastating heartbreak. I couldn't imagine crying my heart out yet again because I had let someone in too deep, yet again.

It took me a while to realise this about myself, but I am extremely sensitive. All it takes is one measly kiss for me to be completely hooked on a guy; and when it's more? I would literally offer you my heart on a platter. After it got smashed enough times, I realised that it was better for me to keep both my heart and my body to myself.

I can talk about how staying celibate helps you "shine your eye" so that you don't end up with the wrong person just because the sex is so good.

I can talk about how there are connections that go deeper than the physical and how volatile it is for you to have those connections with anyone outside of the safety of marriage (it's like starting a fire on your bed and hoping the house wont burn down.)

I can talk about how managing lust when you're single helps you learn discipline so that you don't fall into the temptation to cheat, when you're married – but if you don't find a reason that's important enough for you, you'll just nod and smile and continue as you were.

Personally, I found my reason.

Lack of control is the primary reason why people cheat, and it's the same reason we don't stick to our healthy diets: we haven't found a good enough reason to convince ourselves that it's important.

Understand the facts, understand the truth (sex is not just about the physical release and celibacy is not just about punishing yourself) and find a reason that's important enough to keep you under control.

Okay – but why do we feel loneliness and sexual desire when we're single, if we're not meant to have sex until we're married?

God only stirs up desires in us when He wants to fulfil those desires. This works for every aspect of life: if you suddenly have the desire to help poor people, it's a sign that God wants to use you to help poor people in the world. If you've always had the desire to be an athlete, it's probably a sign that God wants you to work in sports. This is the principle at work when we ask people what their "passion" is; it is a desire for something that lets you know what you were called to do.

Sexual desire is one of the signs that lets us know that God has marriage in His plans for us. It's like what Adam would have felt after God decided that it wasn't good for him to be alone.

However, even though sexual desire is a sign that God has marriage in store for you, it is not a sign that you should go ahead to try to fulfil the desire by yourself. Remember, God led Adam on a teaching and training exercise, then led him into rest, *before* bringing the woman who was the answer to his desires. The process between having a desire and being able to fulfil

111

it is the process of training and equipping, so that we'll be able to handle the fulfilled desires properly.

What does a Happy Marriage look like?

A happy marriage is one where both parties are free to shine their brightest in every area of their lives because they are both in alignment with God and each other.

The two of them are "Naked and Unashamed", able to ask the tough questions even as they cover each others' weaknesses, able to encourage each other to fully thrive without guilt or fear.

Whatever that looks like for each couple may be different, but this is what I believe a happy marriage is.

When considering marriage, is love enough? Should you marry for logic or for love?

Any couple that comes together on physical attraction and emotional feelings alone – without God's input – will find it hard to sustain the realities of marriage on emotions alone.

However, because God is a matchmaker, the process before marriage varies. Some people start off with a logical feeling like, "Right, it's time," while others meet, fall in love and get married.

God may bring emotion first, or He may lead the couple to each other before the feelings grow. The important thing is to make sure we're aligned with God, working with His timing, letting Him lead us, resting and not trying to "work" it out ourselves.

And God is Love, so any couple He brings together will be rooted in His Love.

Is there such a thing as a "Soul Mate" or "The One"?

The first thing to understand, again, is that every individual is complete and whole. We have everything we need to live fruitful lives inside of us, without marriage. Marriage is a unique combination of lives, personalities, lineages and God's Purpose in a particular time for a particular reason, to reflect a unique aspect of God's nature on earth.

If we go back to the analogy of the painter and his colours, we'll see that the painter is free to work any way he wants. He will have an image in His head of what He wants to paint, of course, but anybody who has ever had a plan also knows that plans can change to suit the creator, according to the circumstances.

I believe that if God is like a painter, and He wants a marriage that depicts the colour green, He will look for a yellow and a blue – only yellow and blue will do.

I also believe that, if the painting doesn't turn out exactly how He imagined it, He can choose to change it.

This passage explains it:

Then I went down to the potter's house, and there he was, making something at the wheel. And the vessel that he made of clay was marred in the hand of the potter; so he made it again into another vessel, as it seemed good to the potter to make.

Then the word of the Lord came to me, saying: "O house of Israel, can I not do with you as this potter?" says the Lord. "Look, as the clay *is* in the potter's hand, so *are* you in My hand, O house of Israel! (Jeremiah 18:3-5 NKJV)

So, while I'm not certain where the word "Soul Mate" came from, I do believe that God always has an original plan concerning who He wants us to be joined to in marriage. However, if anything happens to "mar" that plan, He is able to work it together for good and make "another suitable vessel" instead.

What if you don't want to get married at all?

As mentioned earlier, not everyone feels the desire for sex, companionship and marriage.

Sometimes, that happens because of sexual trauma and abuse, and sometimes that happens because that's just how they were created.

God is able to heal pain and/or stir up the desire if He decides that marriage is in His plans for such a person; but it just may be a sign that marriage is not part of His plans for you.

But... there's no Marriage In Heaven!

I'd heard about this "no marriage in Heaven", stuff, and I said to God, "Jesus, why na? Why would I wait all these years with the hope of getting married, when it won't even get to heaven with me? Even Adam and Eve were married, and that was the ideal world; why would You choose to discontinue marriage in heaven?"

Then I realised, there *is* marriage in heaven! It's just not the same as what we have here. The marriage we have on earth is just a symbol and a shadow of marriage in Heaven.

We've talked about God and gender in more depth already, but to summarise, we have two identities as human beings: our identity as Sons of God, and our identity as the Bride of Christ. Our identity as Sons enables us to live on earth and carry out God's assignment, and our identity as Bride enables us to become one with Christ – the same way marriage allows couples to become one.

On earth we become one flesh, in heaven we become one Spirit. Everything that is flesh passes away, but everything that is Spirit is eternal.

As we live out our roles on earth, we learn what we need to step into the fullness of our role in Heaven – so, there *is* marriage in Heaven; we will all be married (joined together) to God in perfect intimacy.

Can God tell you who your spouse is?
This brings us to the next part of my story.

Hearing God

I was doing everything I could to stay in relationship with God. The more I felt like He was interested in the mundane parts of my life, the closer I felt to Him and the easier it was to really be in a relationship with Him. I was still afraid that every time I messed up, something bad would happen, and I still wanted to be married so bad that I wondered if there was still something I was missing in my relationship with Him. I mean, if God was happy with me, didn't that mean He was going to lead me to my husband, already?

But I was still single. And when it came to work and career I still didn't know if I was meant to be a complete creative or find a structured job; I didn't seem to be able to do both, successfully.

One day, my friend's husband started an email thread talking about dreams and their interpretations. He said that God was always speaking to us, which I could believe, but he also said that all our dreams were figurative messages from God. As someone who had always had dreams – and never seen any come to pass – I was sceptical about that. I mean, how would I expect a dream about me jumping on cars or dancing with

Antonio Banderas come to pass? The only dreams I had that seemed to relate to real life were the ones I had when I was under pressure, either around an exam or deadline of some sort, or when I was worried about something. As far as I was concerned, that was just my mind's way of helping me sort through stressful situations, but my friend's husband insisted that dreams were symbolic and that we just had to ask God to teach us how to interpret them. The first step, he said, was to write them down.

When I started writing my dreams down, it was as if Heaven had been waiting for exactly that moment: I received an avalanche of dreams. I would shut my eyes for fifteen minutes and end up with dreams that would take thirty minutes to an hour each to write down and I was overwhelmed; I had no idea what they meant. I enjoy studying symbols in literature and in life in general but the problem with symbols is that they can mean a million things. With Godly dream interpretation, we have to rely entirely on Holy Spirit's leading to understand which one of the millions of symbols are represented by the dream and, since we can't see Holy Spirit and can't always be certain what we're hearing, it makes this process a lot less... substantial.

It was a frustrating process but because I had already started practicing listening to God for little things, I figured I could give Him the permission to take me even deeper.

One day in April of 2015, I woke up from a really long dream that ended with me stepping out of a red car. I described the car as the red version of a friend's car – it was like the LG to my friend's Samsung, a similar design by a more affordable brand.

I didn't need a car at the time and there were so many other symbols I didn't understand in that dream so I thought nothing of it, but by the end of the year, the car I had been using was faulty. I borrowed my brother's car and that gave me issues as well, so I prayed, together with my fellowship group, that I would get a brand new car. I certainly couldn't afford it on my freelancing income, so it would have to be a gift.

It took all the courage I had to ask my father to buy me a car. He isn't the sort of dad who believes in giving gifts for no reason; you had to have earned it through an accomplishment or occasion and he has to agree that you have earned it, or that it was okay for you to have it. His philosophy is simple: if you can't earn it, you shouldn't have it. If you get something you can't earn on your own, it creates a mentality of entitlement.

I completely understood this. I didn't even have a steady income and I hadn't done anything praiseworthy so there was no reason why he should buy me an entire car. Still, I figured the worst he would say was no.

He didn't say no. And, at first, he didn't even give me a hard time. He asked me to do my research on what car I wanted and get back to him, at what point he would reassess my request. I thought I was being practical when I asked for a Corolla but that just happened to be the year when prices skyrocketed; suddenly, the price of a Corolla was the same as a lower-end luxury car. When I told my dad how much it cost, he laughed out loud and that was that.

It wasn't until January the next year that I remembered that I'd seen a red car before. It was a brand I'd never considered, but I figured it was probably cheap enough. I walked into the showroom – just to see – and it was like déjà vu; it had the features I'd seen in my dream and, what's more, there was a sale going on.

Nine months after I'd seen myself step out of a red car at the end of a dream that I still don't understand, I had the exact same car in real life.

I figured it was a good idea to continue writing down my dreams.

"I'm Getting Married in June."

After the red car materialised out of my dreams, I figured God was actually showing me things, so when I suddenly had a feeling that I was getting married in June of the same year – completely out of the blues – I figured there could be something there. It didn't come in a dream or a vision and, I hadn't been asking God for a date or anything; the feeling just came, and it stuck.

It's very likely that it had something to do with the fact that I was turning thirty in June that year. I'm not sure why, but thirty is the universal pressure point for single women. However, because I'd had years of practice being alone and was growing more confident in my singleness, I thought I had bypassed the dread that comes with being unmarried at thirty.

"My mum got married at thirty," I used to say, "and she had five healthy children. Therefore, I refuse to be under pressure until I'm at least her age."

So, when this "feeling" came, I was filled with a certainty and hope that felt like faith, not pressure. And whenever I would doubt and beg God to snap me out of my foolishness, something encouraging would happen. I took those little encouraging things as signs that God was listening: He saw my heart and wanted me to keep believing.

Like, this one time. It was a few months into the year, around March, when I suddenly decided I wanted a yellow bag. I would be getting ready to go out to a meeting, sigh dramatically in my room and say, "But, God, where's my yellow bag? You know I need a yellow bag." Then I would pick up another perfectly good bag

121

and go about my business. I did this for weeks, every single time I went out.

Then, one day, it hit me that I couldn't possibly get married in June. It was March already and I wasn't even seeing anyone, so how could it happen? Maybe I could meet someone in June, but I could not honestly expect to get married in June.

I allowed the practical difficulty of the situation get to me and I cried, "Lord, if this is a stupid thing to hold on to, please help me let go of it. I don't have anything to prove by holding on to faith for something that's not going to happen!"

I was fully prepared to have a pity party and stay in my room all day but I had to go out to a meeting at some point, so I dragged myself out of bed and got ready. I looked at my not-yellow bag and sighed; all this foolishness I was engaging in this year. Just because I got the car from the dream didn't mean I should run around being silly.

I went downstairs, told my mum I was going out and started to walk out of the door when she said, "Have you seen that my yellow bag?"

I froze.

"Your what?"

"My yellow bag. Daddy bought it for me but it's too big."

I was speechless.

"It's like the one you're carrying," she continued, "I just remembered it when I saw this your bag."

The next day, my mum brought her brand new yellow bag – still in the dust bag – up to my room.

Tell me that wasn't a sign. Just tell me! God had had a yellow bag for me, all this time. He had just kept it safe with my mum until the time was right.

In fact, let's break this bag miracle down:

God knew He wanted me to have a yellow bag, so He stirred up the desire in my heart. I started going up and down saying, "I need a yellow bag," out of nowhere. Then when I had come to the end of myself, entered into a deep sleep, He brought the bag to me. This was my sign! My husband was around the corner. Hallelujah!

I didn't get married in June.

I didn't even meet anyone in June. Or July, or August, or September, or – well, I'm still single as I write this, so, yeah.

But something else did happen in June.

I don't know how to write this part without chuckling.

Let's pretend we're all friends and we're sitting around in someone's bedroom, having a sleepover, just chatting into the night. Someone says, "Omotayo, give us the gist of what happened in June!"

And I say, "Okay okay."

"Don't summarise it, o, give us the gist in full!"

"Okay, but before I get to June I have to go back a bit," I say.

"Go back as far as you want! We're listening."

"So, one day on Instagram, I stumbled on a certain celebrity's posts and he was talking about God, about being saved and telling everyone to give their lives to Jesus, everything. I went to his page and saw that he had been posting about God since last year! I followed him immediately."

"You that you've always liked him, are you sure you followed him for God?"

I laugh, "Leave me. At least, that's why I'm following him now."

In real life, I was stunned to find out that this celebrity was now preaching the gospel unashamedly, and on his social media page, no less. I couldn't get over it and I kept sharing his posts with my friends.

One day, one of my friends said to me, "This one that you're always talking about him. Shouldn't we hook you up?"

"No," I laughed, "If I wanted to be hooked up with him, there are so many connections. I can even hook myself up!"

"Hm, are you sure?" she pressed.

"Let me pray about it," I said, mostly to shake her off, but when she said, "Ha, all this time, you've not prayed about it??" I wondered, should I have been praying?

But what would I have been praying for? "God, I might have a crush on a guy that every human female has a crush on, so, is he my June husband?" That seemed ridiculous.

I put my phone down and sat with God for a minute, amused but curious.

"Lord, I don't really know what to say."

Then I felt a nudge: "Write your list," God seemed to whisper.

Another back-story:

I had actually met someone in December, the year before. I fell willingly and easily. He was the radiance of my spec and the exact imprint of my desires in a husband.

I said to God, "Wow, I didn't know You still had men like this around! Thank You for keeping this one single for me."

But then just like that, the romance was over. In a week, we had stopped talking. It was like a dream that never happened... but I guess I couldn't let it go because in April – just a few weeks after I had received my yellow bag – I found myself standing in the valley of dry bones, wondering, "Lord, can these bones live? Can this dead romance come alive?"

I didn't wait for His answer; I prophesied to myself that they surely could and gave myself a sign to look out for. "Verily, verily, if thou doth texteth him and if he doth reply, surely, the bones shall rise again."

So I sent him a belated Easter greeting in April and, lo, he doth replyeth.

We started chatting again; we met up for drinks and all the feelings came back. He asked me what happened, why I disappeared and I was so happy we were talking again that I didn't even get upset about the fact that he'd made it my fault.

We kept talking for a few weeks, you know, long midnight calls, painting pictures of a potential future... but our pictures didn't match.

One day I said to him, "I think you want the kind of babe who always does her nails, has her hair on fleek and all that."

He said to me, "But you always do your nails."

I did, sometimes. But sometimes, I didn't. I didn't want to be with a guy who would wake up one day and say, "This is not the woman I married; the woman I married always does her nails. You've started letting yourself go."

One day I told him that my friend and I had planned to rent a flat together but she got married before it could happen. He said, "Is it this same freelance work you wanted to use to move?"

It was. I knew it wasn't practical, I knew I needed a plan to earn more money, but I didn't want to be married to someone who came at it from the problem and not looking toward the solution.

I'm painting this picture to show that there was nothing wrong with what he said or what he wanted, it just didn't fit with where I was and what I wanted – he wanted a high achiever who had a structured career and always looked hot. I wanted a supportive and encouraging man who believed in my creative dreams more than I did and worked with me to achieve them.

And, all the while, I kept feeling the nudge to write a list. It almost seems as if God was saying, "Omotayo, you need to know what you want so that you'll be able to identify what's important and what's not."

But I felt guilty. "Christian girls don't write lists! All we're supposed to want is a God-fearing man. We're not supposed to have preferences or be particular, we're supposed to be meek and patient."

"But there are things you want," God would nudge. "I know what you like, you know what you like. Why don't you just write them down?"

"No. Christian girls don't have lists. We trust the Lord – that is the only List we need."

I met up with a dear friend in the middle of it and we spent hours catching up on a year's worth of gist. I mentioned the fact that I kept getting the nudge to write a list, but that I was rejecting it because it went against every "single woman" admonition I'd heard – you know, those sermons where the pastor says, "Some of you ladies, you're still single because you're waiting for the perfect man. Your list is so long, it's only Jesus that can marry you! You better stop waiting or you'll find yourself still attending single meetings when you're fifty!"

But my friend said, "God told some of my friends to write lists, too! And now, they're married."

What? Could this be real?

She nodded, "Yes. In fact, He said to one of them, 'If I say I'm going to do abundantly above all that you can ask or imagine, how will you know that I've indeed done above all you asked or imagined if you haven't written it down?'"

Take a minute.

Read it again.

Breathe.

You mean we actually serve a God who actually wants to exceed our expectations?

Let's go back to the celebrity guy.

We're now in June, I'm sitting on my bed wondering what kind of prayer to pray and God says, "Write your list."

It's as if He was saying the same thing, "Omotayo, you need to know what you want so that you'll be able to identify what's important and what's not." But now, He added, "That way, you'll know whether this celebrity thing is just a social media crush or if you actually want it to be something more. Then you'll know what to pray."

Grudgingly, I agreed to write a list.

"But it's only going to have a few things – not even up to a page!" I said, and started writing. My people, I was still writing till I filled the page and turned it over to the other side.

Do you know what happened next? I looked at it, was so filled with shame and self-condemnation for writing such a long list that I held it up and was about to tear it up. I was almost in tears.

"I just want someone who loves God and loves me! I don't want to be picky!"

Just as I would have torn it, I felt a very stern scolding in my heart – as if God was looking me in the eye like an angry parent in front of a recalcitrant toddler, saying, "If you *dare*!"

I shuddered.

"Ah ahn, there's no one here," I shook it off, "Why am I afraid? It's just my imagination."

I felt the nudge once more, like a Yoruba Mother with her hand on her hip who has now stood up in anger because her child is testing her patience. Any moment now, she would send her older son to cut a stick from the garden because clearly, the only way this child would understand was via a whooping.

I tried to compromise.

"Okay, Let me just rewrite it into a different notebook," I said.

My plan was to shrink it down to one page and edit out the other unnecessary things. At least I didn't tear it, right?

Listen, God showed me. I ended up writing *pages*.

I started begging. "Please, please don't let me get to a hundred items, Lord! I'm sorry I tried to trick You. Please, I'm sorry!"

And God relented. We stopped at seventy.

And so, it was in June that I wrote my list, my very detailed list of who my husband was. It wasn't so much a list of what I wanted when I fantasised about the perfect man; it was a description of who God wanted me to be with.

It had some fickle things on it, of course, but it was mostly an indepth character description. It had things like, "Someone who has a respectful relationship with his dad. Not because it has always been perfect, but because he has gone through his rebellious phase and has come out of it." And, "His mum loves me. His sisters love me. I am like another sibling to them. His father loves me. His mum and my mum become great friends."

I wrote, "His purpose and my purpose work together – speaking God's truth on public platforms." "He has a purpose to start a business that will make an impact in Nigeria, Africa and the world."

But I also wrote, "He's a reformed bad boy, he loves dancing, he gives excellent massages" and, "I find him irresistibly attractive."

I even chose a birth month, age and what school he went to! My reasoning was, I didn't want a snobbish IJGB. I also didn't want someone who had never experienced an education outside the country, so my compromise was, "Someone who went to a Federal Government school in Lagos – at least for secondary school, maybe even university – and then went abroad after."

I said to God, "I know many items are flexible, You can do whatever You like; I'm just telling You what I would like."

And God said, "Finally, you're being honest about what you really want, instead of pretending to be a holy Christian sister."

After I wrote the list I realised I didn't need to pray about the celebrity.

I also realised that the guys I had liked in the past had had some of the items on the list – and not just the fickle things. Some were really intelligent – but weren't kind. Some were kind – but didn't love God. Some were kind and intelligent, but were still angry with authority and hadn't learnt the value of mentorship… etc.

I say that to say this: there's a reason why I was drawn to the men I'd liked in the past. I had seen a glimmer of something special in them. They had essentially good hearts but were still going through their process, as I was. As I still am.

In the same way, I believe that there's a reason why you were drawn to your exes; you saw something special, like the flash of a diamond buried in the ground. The fact that your heart was broken after it ended doesn't mean you made a mistake; it just means the two of you weren't in the same place at the same time.

It's all about timing: the fact that an orange isn't ripe enough to eat doesn't mean it's a bad orange. You and your spouse must be ripe, ready and in agreement at the time you decide to enter into a marriage, otherwise there'll be a struggle.

While everyone I've loved has had essentially good hearts, they weren't necessarily ready to be vulnerable or committed or purposeful at the time that I was practicing vulnerability and learning the importance of purpose and needing commitment – and vice versa. Two people can't walk together on a journey if they don't agree.

I hope you are able to forgive all those who broke your heart in the past. I hope you can see that it just wasn't meant to be, at the time. I hope you can allow yourself to grow and soar and be all you that you can be – because that's when you'll find someone who perfectly matches the real you, at the right time.

Turning Thirty

So I had written my list. I had clarity. I was excited; I was going to meet my husband soon. But it was still June and I was still turning thirty and I was still completely single.

I didn't admit how disappointed I was until a few days to my birthday; I hadn't even planned anything because I wanted to plan a wedding, instead. Listen, I had a wedding book, I had chosen my asoebi colours, I had decided to have cousins on my train instead of friends because I have so many best friends... I was all set. I had even been preparing my parents to expect a small wedding for a few years and my dad seemed to have gotten comfortable with the idea. (I've since changed my mind. After this journey, I want everyone to celebrate my wedding with me! But don't tell them I said so.)

Three days to my birthday, I was watching a movie and something sad happened in the movie, so I cried –

– and cried and cried and cried and cried. When I realised I wasn't actually crying about the movie, I knelt by my bed and wept some more.

"Why am I still single? Why did You make me believe June would happen? Why didn't I even meet anyone this year? Why did You continue to encourage me? I knew this would happen! You just strung me along! You could have let me down earlier! Am I even supposed to get married?"

Then I went deeper.

"Why am I still here, in my parents' house? Why am I broke? My clothes are old and worn out. I can barely afford to have a nice meal in a nice restaurant; I can definitely not afford to travel. If You weren't going to sort out my marriage, why haven't You sorted out my finances?"

And deeper, still.

"This rubbish creative gift. Why didn't You make me structured and disciplined? Why didn't You give me the desire to work in a bank? I could have been anything else and I would have had a successful career. Instead I'm here, in my feelings, trying to make a living from being creative and failing woefully at it. Why is this my life? Why is this my path?"

I don't know how, but I finally stopped crying. I probably had a headache from crying so much. I got up from my kneeling position and sat on the edge of my bed, looking over my room.

And then I felt that nudge.

"Look around you," it seemed like God was saying. "Look at all the clothes hanging on that wardrobe. They may be old, but no one knows that except you. You have all the clothes you need."

Hmm.

"Look at your shoes. Yes, they're worn out. But you still have one or two good ones and you don't go out every single day, so you're okay."

Hmmm.

"You have everything you need for where you are. I cover you. You will never go out and feel ashamed of your clothes."

"But…" I thought. "Like, why do I need the miracle of not being ashamed, if I could have the miracle of consistent cashflow? Or the miracle of a husband? This was not where I thought I would be when I dreamed about my life at thirty."

And God said, "You can't hold yourself to standards that your sixteen year old self set for you. She didn't know what life was going to bring. She had no idea what the journey was going to look like."

Woosh.

"*You* know what life has been like. When you look back at the unexpected deviations in the journey, did you handle them well?"

"I think I did," I thought, "Maybe I could have done better, but I did the best I could at the time."

"You can only do as well as what you know to do. And each time, you made the best decision you could. You handled life the best way you knew. That's the most important thing."

I tried to allow myself to hear this.

"Omotayo, you have done your best. Your sixteen-year-old self would be proud of you if she knew how you handled the unexpected twists and turns of life. But you can't continue to live your life by the standards and expectations that *she* set. Release yourself from that."

I sat there, breathing, taking it in.

"Look around you again. You live in a nice house in a nice neighbourhood. You're not making money but you're not starving, far from it. Your parents are together. There's no family drama. You have your privacy, and freedom to go on this strange journey I've set you on. Omotayo, you're good."

I'm good?

"You have everything you need for where you are. You have everything you need to take the next step. You have everything *I* think you need to be everything you need to be, Omotayo."

Everything changed, that day.

The idea that I was not a disappointment to God and I wasn't even a disappointment to myself changed my perspective.

I started to look at those "worn out" clothes on the rack with new appreciation. My shoes, my room, my bed, even my mosquito net. Everything was new and beautiful.

"I'm turning thirty! And I've done alright for myself, so far!" I thought.

Before then, I wouldn't have believed that it was possible to be free of the burden of unmet expectations, but I was. I wasn't disappointed in myself anymore and, most importantly, God wasn't disappointed in me.

I turned on worship music and danced. This time, when I cried, it was with so much joy. I was finally living up to my name, the one who is worthy of joy.

***

Dear Singleton, forgive yourself for all the mistakes you made, all the time you wasted, all the things you didn't achieve.

God is not disappointed in you, so don't be disappointed in yourself.

Don't be afraid to accept that you are good enough; it doesn't mean that you have lower standards of success, it just means that you understand that there's nothing you can do about the time you've lost; but there's so much you can do with the time you still have.

So, you didn't start at twenty. So, your mates have done xyz at this age. So, your juniors are catching up with you. Forgive yourself. Forgive God. Forgive your exes for breaking your heart and redirecting your path; and walk boldly into all the possibility that today holds.

As the saying goes, whenever you wake up is your morning. Wake up. It's morning. You can start now. There is still so much more... enter into it.

"God Said He's My Husband"

Thirty was my best birthday yet. I was never ashamed of my age after that; I was so proud of myself and of my life – the good, bad and all of it.

I went for a praise concert the night before and rang in my thirtieth year singing and dancing and praising God. I invited a few friends over for small chops and pictures. Another friend brought props, so it looked like I'd planned it! My pictures looked intentional. I was so genuinely full of joy.

Later in the evening, we all went to have drinks at this restaurant and the celebrity was there! My friends and I kept giggling. I was free of that imagination, as well.

I was so happy to be thirty.

One day, when 2016 had almost ended, I had something like a dream. In it, I heard a date. I remember reaching out from sleep to grab my phone, write it down and go back to sleep, and remembering nothing of it – but I woke up angry.

I tried to act like nothing was happening for days, but I was essentially giving God the cold shoulder. Then in January the next year, my friend led a group to read the book, "Good Morning, Holy Spirit," by Benny Hinn.

In one of the chapters, he described Holy Spirit as a sensitive Being who would wait – or sulk – in the background until you turned finally noticed. I thought, "That's silly, God isn't a petulant girlfriend. If Holy Spirit wants your attention, Holy Spirit knows how to get it."

The funny thing was, it felt like God was showing me that Holy Spirit *did* want my attention, but I was the one sulking.

Sometime in there, I decided to talk. And I exploded.

"Why would You give me another date, again, after what happened last year?! I don't know if this is a Word, a nudge, a sign or my imagination, but why would You keep giving me these vague clues when You know I'm just going to hope again and get disappointed again?!"

I was angry because, in that dream that I'd had that night, I had written, "I'm getting married on August 7."

In May, that year, another dear friend of mine invited me to his house. He had just got married. I got there a bit early and chatted with his wife, who was also a friend.

At some point she asked, "You, *nko*, is there anyone?"

I smiled patiently, "No, there isn't, but I feel like God and I have an understanding. Like, if he walks in here right now, I feel like I'll know who he is and we'll just be like, 'oh, hi! Finally.'"

And then a guy walked in.

I shook it off and said a barely polite hello.

We ended up talking a bit later. He would say something and God would nudge me about something on my list. Something random like, "I'm working on this project I'm very passionate about," and I would feel the nudge, *"Project that can change Nigeria, Africa and the world! Tick."*

Or, "I used to smoke and drink a lot, and I felt like I needed to find a relationship with God for myself," and a nudge, *"Reformed bad boy! Tick."*

"Calm down, Omotayo," I scolded myself. "The guy is just making conversation. Remember, closed until God opens."

No numbers were exchanged, no interest was declared and I went home.

One day in June, I had just done my first ever Instagram Live chat on the topic, "How To Be Single" (wink). It had gone really well and I was pleased.

And then I woke up with a jolt in the middle of the night from a dream where I had seen this guy and myself picking out outfits because we were getting ready to get married.

I wasn't even angry when I woke up. "I must have been more interested in him than I realised," I chuckled, and went about my day.

A week later, my friend, the one whose kitchen I'd been standing in when the guy walked in, called me. Technically, I'd been on the phone with her brother and she took the phone from him.

"Omotayo, do you believe God can tell you who your husband is?"

My heart started beating.

"Yes, I do," I said.

"What if I tell you God told me who your husband is?"

Thump, thump, thump!

"Who did God say?" And I held my breath, waiting to hear his name, because I already knew; God had told me, too.

Then she said someone else's name.

I was so relieved, I laughed and laughed.

"You're wicked," she teased, "You don't like my friend."

This friend she was referring to was a guy she had tried to link me up with, the year before (after I turned thirty.) There were no sparks from my end, even though it felt really weird because he was clearly willing to commit and I was the one who didn't want to "go on the journey".

When she said his name I knew it was absolutely impossible that God said he was my husband and I was relieved.

"And he really liked you, o," she said.

I laughed it off. "Leave that one, please."

Then her voice became serious and she said, "It's not him. I was just teasing," and my heart stopped all over again because I knew whose name she was going to say.

When she did say it, I was calm.

"Are you sure you're not just saying it because you saw the two of us together and think we'll be a good match?" I'd told myself that newly married people were so caught up in the bubble of new love that they were always looking for other couples to set up.

But she said, "No. God told me in April."

That took the breath out of my lungs.

When I got off the phone I went back to the dream I had had, barely a week earlier. It was long and complex and the only part I understood was the part where we were talking about what we were going to wear for our wedding.

I thought about the other dream with the date and looked at the calendar. August 7 was a Monday. "Okay," I thought, "Small wedding, it is."

Then I panicked.

How was this happening to me?

Was it a good thing or a bad thing?

Why did God tell me before telling him?
What was I supposed to do with the information?

Are You ___ Enough?

This was *not* how I wanted it to happen.

I mean, yes, I said I didn't want to choose for myself. Yes, I wanted God to choose. Yes, I said my heart would be closed until He opened it, but I wanted the guy to come to me! I didn't want to be the weird one who had to convince a guy to want me.

I went back to my list, that glorious description of the man with God's heart who had been prepared for me as Adam was for Eve, and I faltered.

A thought flitted across my mind: "If this guy on your list shows up in the flesh, would you even be good enough for him?"

That thought took me by surprise. As far as I was concerned, I was a very confident woman. I was smart and pretty and I had a good heart. God had been working on me and I was becoming more peaceful, less judgmental; more open, less clique-ish. Sure, I wasn't making money but I was still okay. Right? And, I mean, I couldn't brag about my eforiro or my jollof, but I could cook enough to feed a home. And, anyway, what kind of husband would only want me for my cooking skills? That wasn't someone I wanted to be with. But if this man was truly everything on the list, shouldn't I try to be better for him?

What if he needs me to help out with the finances sometimes? That's not an unreasonable request. What if we go through a rough patch and I can't even just take a steady job long enough to help because "I'm not wired like that"? What kind of irresponsible wife and mother would refuse to make that sacrifice for her family? If I was the one meeting a guy who said he was waiting on God to figure out finances, would I like it? But, no, I can have double standards and want a husband who already has it figured out.

In a matter of hours, my façade of confidence crumbled.

I felt like I wasn't good enough. I didn't know enough, hadn't achieved enough, wasn't well rounded enough, wasn't rich enough.

"So, if we get married, now, is he the one who'd now have to buy me a whole new wardrobe? Why can't I even buy myself new clothes?!"

Just like that, we were back to the insecurities of the past.

And that's where God started. Faced with the actual possibility of an actual marriage, I was scared that any man who got deep enough would see my mess and leave me – or, even if he couldn't leave me, he would be miserable trying to love me enough to love myself.

As I write, I'm reminded that this was the same fear I'd had with my ex. Time had passed, I had formed a deeper relationship with God and I was content with my life – for the most part – but I still hadn't resolved the main issue. In my dad's words, I still didn't know how to receive love.

So I gave it, instead.

Well, I tried. I poured it out on this guy. I prayed for him every single day; asked God to give me prophetic declarations to make over his life. We weren't even in contact – no numbers had been exchanged, and I didn't even know for sure if he had been informed about the wife God was keeping for him in the backyard. I just prayed and declared God's Word over him every single day. Words about his career, his heart, his childhood pain, his flaws and weaknesses, his relationships with his friends, toxic exes – God literally started downloading all that information to me and I prayed and prayed for him.

Then I had a fear, what if I'd never be able to move to marriage until I talked about Singleness? What if God needed me to teach about being Single before He would finally be happy enough with me to let me get married? I had to make sure I ticked all the boxes and gave God zero reason to deny me of this miraculous marriage, and so I started doing the weekly How To Be Single live chats, sharing all the things God had been teaching me about the right mindset toward singleness, being whole: perfect and complete, lacking nothing.

I didn't realise it at the time, but I was hoping I could prove that I was worthy of love by giving it – giving it to my online audience, hopefully giving it to God through that act of service and, most importantly, giving it to this guy by praying for him, constantly.

It was fulfilling, it really was. God finally had my full attention and He started to reveal deep things to me. The deeper the revelation I got about this guy, the deeper God would dig into my own heart. Again, it was fulfilling, but my thought process was faulty: God didn't need my penance in order to bless me. He makes the sun shine on the righteous and the unrighteous and He makes the rain fall on both, in equal measure. His blessings make us rich and add no sorrow or toil or stress to us – we do not pay God in service and worship in order to receive His goodness; He is good to us because He is a good God.

One day, God told me that I had been abused as a child.

I scoffed. "Abeg it's not by force to have an abuse story, Lord. This is not relevant to my journey."

The nudge, again, "If you can believe all these things I'm telling you about someone you don't even know, why can't you believe this?"

"Let's just leave it, please, there's no need for this extra drama." I wasn't having it.

But neither was God. Somehow, I found myself saying, "Fine, okay, tell me what happened."

And He did.

I was a mess, that day; not so much because of what happened but because of who did it. As God replayed it all to me, He also gave me the understanding of why they had done it. For one person, it was because he had seen someone he admired do it and, even though there's always an inner voice telling us what's right from wrong, it's easy for that voice to be replaced by the louder voice that says, "But if he can do it, it must be okay."

For the other person, he'd excused his actions with logic, "I just love her so much. If I feel like this and I'm not hurting her, it must be okay."

But even though I sobbed, I said, "God, I understand. I forgive them. Now can we just forget about it? Please don't make me have to confront them or fight or anything. I'm okay; I'm living my life. We're all happy and alive and good so, please, just leave it."

It took a little while, but God left it. Every few months He would nudge me again to see if I was ready to really address it, not just act like a Holy Christian Sister. It took me a few more years before I could, and even then –

But the reason He had brought it up was to show me where the feeling of not being good enough had come from – not because my life was ruined by it, not because there was a curse over me because of it, not because He wanted a dramatic confrontation, but to give me information.

The bible says that we perish for lack of knowledge. Like, if you don't know that you can use a microwave to warm your food, you may spend hours trying to use firewood. In the process, you may get splinters in your fingers, get smoke in your eye and really just end up spending longer than you needed to to address a simple issue.

Abuse doesn't ruin our lives. Nothing is strong enough to destroy a child of God. However, abuse does distort the lens with which we see our lives. It suggests to us like a gossiping friend, "Maybe it happened because you're not good enough. Maybe it happened because you did something wrong. Maybe if you hadn't worn that or said that or gone there, it wouldn't have happened. Maybe you always make bad decisions. Maybe people will always take advantage of you and there's nothing you can do about it. Maybe this is just how life is."

And if you dare complain about your experience, the friends of this voice attack, "Eh ehn? So, are you the only one who experienced something bad in your life?

Well done o, if you like, stay stuck here and be whining about it. Can't you see your mates, thriving? So if you had experienced something worse, would you have died? Snap out of it, *jo*!"

The problem with these voices is that they pull us in opposite directions: on the one hand, it's your fault. On the other, get over it. We spend our lives going from one extreme to the other, trying to be normal, but neither of these perspectives come from God.

God says,

"My son. My daughter. My child. Bring your pain to Me. Acting like it didn't happen won't fix it. Trying to make them pay won't fix it, either. No one on earth can fix it. Bring it to Me.

"I will restore what was stolen. Your sense of value; that deep knowledge every child is born with that lets them know that they are fully and entirely loved. The freedom to be who you were meant to be without wondering if someone else will take advantage – that's what they stole.

"Cry to Me. I will fix it. I am your source of value. I am your freedom. I am Love, and I will fill you up so much that you will have enough running over to give – even to the ones who hurt you.

"Just come."

What You Bring To The Table

When the question, "What do you bring to the table?" comes up around single people, the conversation tends toward achievement and financial contribution.

Men feel pressure to have enough money to provide lavish lifestyles for their families and they lash out at the women as if to say, "Bring your own; let's share the burden equally."

Women, in turn, come under the same pressure, with the effect that the burden gets compounded rather than divided. Whenever you place a burden on something that wasn't meant to carry it, you create a bigger problem.

Let me address this, quickly: there's a difference between the *weight of responsibility* and a person's *ability*. That a ten year old is *able* to drive is one thing; however, that child cannot handle the *weight of the responsibility* of driving, which includes consideration for others, ability to focus on one thing without getting distracted, ability to multitask, to make life and death decisions in split seconds, etc. Yes, a ten year old can drive if they're tall enough, if you need someone to

153

move the car or if there's an emergency, however, it will never be that child's permanent responsibility.

In a marriage union between a husband and a wife, the husband is meant to shoulder the weight of the responsibility of provision and protection. That a wife is more than able to generate surplus income is not in question, however, the woman is not supposed to carry that weight.

In the same way, the fact that a man is able to nurture does not mean he is meant to carry the weight of the responsibility to nurture in a marriage.

The two individuals will often and very frequently be required to play both roles but, again, there is a difference between ability, and weight of responsibility.

Once someone's value in a relationship comes into question, distrust and insecurity arise. Thoughts like, "When we started talking, you thought I was valuable enough, but now I need to prove myself to you?" "So you've had enough of me and if I don't prove my value, you'll leave me?" "How about all the time I spend taking care of your needs; how do you quantify that?"

Marriage is a partnership of two people who should be aware that the mere presence of the other is a valuable addition to their lives.

My Bethel Church Daddies-in-the-Lord, Kris Valotton and Bill Johnson have quoted this saying a few times, "God doesn't make a person and then put a dream inside them; He has a dream, then He wraps a person around that dream."

God didn't first make you, and then start figuring out what to do with you. He had a plan, *then* He created the perfect human being to execute that plan.

You are the only individual in the universe that can do what you can do.

It is God who works in you to bring the purpose He created you for, to pass. Every mistake and misstep is what qualifies you for the thing(s) He wants you to do. He created you – your life, your history, your quirks, your personality, your country, your lineage – and put you where you are *so that* you would be equipped to do the thing He's working out in you.

There is no delay in God; there is only delay outside of God. And once you get back in with Him, the Creator of Time, He simply works everything together, instructing Time to adjust itself to accommodate His Child.

The church talks about "missing it" a lot. We focus on mistakes and missteps, as if God did not already factor all our sins into account before bringing Jesus to die for them. Like, He wrote the script and played out the scenes, saw all the plot holes and bad acting, the bad attitude, habits, addictions, mistakes, accidents, the evil in the world, the bad guy's strategy, every single thing. He calculated how much all those mistakes would cost,

155

if someone ever tried to pay the ransom for the entire created universe and figured, "It's only the blood of the One who Created them that can fix this mess."

Then he thought, "But how?"

And Jesus said, "Send Me. I'll take on their flesh so that I will be able to pay in the same currency as what they have lost."

Then Jesus gave perfect righteousness in exchange for sin and our criminal records were wiped clean.

After all this, why do we still think we have anything to contribute? There is literally no amount of atonement and sacrifice and service in church that will contribute even a dot to the already perfect and finished work that Jesus did, once and for all. Our role is to accept the gift, instead of snobbing it and saying, "I don't trust this kind of God. There's no such thing as a free gift."

Maybe in the world, but in God? Everything you are is His free gift to you.

As a whole, perfect and complete individual, you are altogether beautiful and there is no flaw in you. You don't need to pitch yourself to someone else so that they'll see your value. You don't need to be a hustler or paper-chasing money-maker to show your future spouse that you have something to contribute. What you bring to the table is yourself – but you need to believe it.

You are valuable. Just by being born, you are valuable. Just look at a couple who've been waiting to have a child and you can see that. Your life is valuable to the world. You may not know it, yet, but you knew it when you were born. Life may have taught you hard lessons that made you forget it, but the fact that a diamond is treated like granite doesn't make it any less a diamond.

The idea behind bringing something to the table in a relationship is tied to the idea that we have to *do* something to prove our value: you must have a certain amount of money to show that you're valuable. You must have a certain kind of exposure, come from a certain family, drive a certain car, have a certain job. That is all incorrect.

I believe in being rich and successful, I believe it can be Godly and righteous and holy, even. But I am so confident that it is not a measure of the value God has placed on us, it is only a measure of how much we believe, receive and respond to Him.

I had a conversation with my dad, once, that illustrated the idea very simply.

Years ago, back when Barack Obama was still president of the United states, I was having one of those days where I'd been feeling bad about not understanding how money works and not earning enough. I said to my dad, "I've always thought that the value of what I did had to be measured by how much I make, and if I don't make money then my work is not valuable."

He said, back, "Of course that's not true; look at Obama! He's not the richest man in America, but he's certainly the most valuable."

It's not about your money, it's not about your pedigree, it's not about your activity. It's about who you are: your gifts, talents, exposure, experience – and the courage you have to assert your value without being afraid that someone will judge you or take advantage of you. Remember that your value can't finish, and give yourself permission to live.

Falling Apart

Every single morning, I woke up with this guy, my amazing husband-to-be, on my mind. I constantly had dreams, revelations and prophetic words about him. I entered fully into the position of a wife, fighting for him in prayer whenever God showed me that he was going through a tough time, declaring God's Words over him, all of that. I didn't know I had this warrior prayer woman in me. I looked at myself with new eyes; I was kinda proud of myself.

And, all the while, we hadn't even spoken to each other.

One day, I was writing in my journal, chatting with God as I always did, when God said, "Get his number, call him and tell him."

Backstory:

I had two other friends at the time who'd had clear words about who God said their husbands were. When they confided in me – before I'd experienced it – I thought they were crazy. I mean, I knew they weren't choosing to be crazy, but the situation was crazy. I remember saying, "God, why are You doing this to Your daughters? Please bring them out of this craziness."

The joke was entirely on me.

It got to a time when God prompted one of them to let her guy know, but she was too scared to do it. By the time she'd mustered the courage to tell him, weeks had passed and he had gotten engaged. He'd still had feelings for her, at the time, but it didn't change his decision.

When this happened, I was so angry. I was angry with her for letting fear hold her back. I was angry with him for claiming to care about her and still choosing not to marry her. I was angry with God for seeing it all and allowing it to happen.

With all this righteous anger, I couldn't ignore my own instruction when it came. I would never have forgiven myself if I'd ignored it or acted like it was my imagination and the same thing happened to me.

Petrified within an inch of my sanity, I got his number, called him and told him.

He took it very well. Gracious and kind, he heard me out without drama or mockery.

Then I said, "I've been praying for you since – not praying, like, God bring my husband or anything, but, like, God reveals things to me about your work, life, things like that. And I pray."

Very calmly, he asked, "Do you have any of these prayers written down?"

"Yeah, I have journals full of prayers. I write them all down."

"Do you mind sending them to me, please?" he asked.

Oh-kay?

"Sure," I said.

I would probably have forgotten to follow up and actually send the prayers. At the time, I didn't think it was important. As far as I was concerned, I had done my part and God would do the rest.

"At least, if anything happens now, it won't be my fault," I thought, proud of myself for my courage – and ready to blame God if anything bad happened.

But immediately after I made the call, I happened to have a meeting. I had never met the young lady before and she was late to the meeting, so by the time she showed up, I was an emotional wreck and I blurted out the entire story to her.

Calmly, she shut her notebook, put her pen aside and proceeded to tell me a crazy story about how she met the guy she was dating at the time. My eyes widened in awe.

Then she said, "Oya, text him, text him."

"Text him, what?"

"The prayers! You better text him the prayers."

"Oh. Okay…"

"Do it now!"

"They're not on my phone. I have to go home and look through my journals."

"What are you waiting for? Go home!"

I laughed. "No, let's have our meeting. I'll do it when I get home."

"Are you sure?"

"Yes, I promise."

I randomly picked out three or four prayers, typed them up with the dates of each prayer included, and sent them off.

Hours later, he replied, "Wow. These are accurate. Down to the date and topic."

Turns out that he journalled his prayers, too. He looked at the dates of my prayers and saw that they matched his.

My excitement levels were through the roof!

My Faithful God had done it! Look at the evidence; glaring evidence. Yes, August had passed, but we could still get married this year! Hallelujah!

We started talking often, then a lot. I had already chosen to love him when God sent the word but now I fell in love with him. It was glorious because I was not afraid of getting hurt; God had chosen, so I was safe.

I was still getting prophetic words about his work, his life, his friendships. It was even spookier now; I would pray something and it would literally happen. He marvelled. I marvelled. I never knew God could be so sweet.

So, whenever we had little fights (by which I mean, whenever I prompted him to commit) they surprised me.

"Lord, why isn't he getting the memo? Why is he still doubting when You're constantly confirming this?"

Those "little fights" culminated in a conversation where I essentially told him to go off and find his confirmation by himself, since he was clearly not sure.

He went, and never came back.

***

What happens when a skyscraper falls down with you in it? I cannot sufficiently convey the pain that followed the breakdown of this God dream. I asked myself a million questions what went wrong. I continued to pray for him, continued to get revelation, continued to believe that he would come back.

Then, one day, I had a dream where I saw him propose to another woman.

I rebuked the dream! I declared my victory! And yet, one day, almost two years after we'd stopped talking, he called to let me know he was engaged. He had met her a few months before. He had prayed about his decision, he'd also asked trusted friends to pray with him, and God had given His blessing.

I had spent the entire time hoping but, now, it was over.

Did God Really Say?

To say I was disappointed with God would be an epic understatement. God, the same God who had wooed me with His love, given me revelation of things I could never have known, spoken to me, led me, guided me. My God who was my Friend, had seen this coming, and still, He let me fall. In fact, He wanted me to fall. That was it; that must be it. Why else would He sit on His Throne and let this happen?

I thought about our agreement, that my heart would be shut until He opened it. He opened it, alright, just to smash it to pieces.

I tried to cry my heart out until it bled all over the floor but God wouldn't let me; I could only cry enough to ease the pressure, but He wouldn't let me fall apart. I was mad at that, too. I wanted the sweet comfort of depression so deep, it would show Him not to play with my feelings like that, again.

I wanted to be a wreck to show God that I did not care about Him anymore. Since being faithful led me here, I might as well try unfaithfulness. But He wouldn't let me.

So I switched tactics: took a deep breath and pulled myself together.

"Omotayo, be rational," I admonished myself, "God is good, so He couldn't have done this to you. If He didn't do it to you, you must have done it to yourself. You must have misunderstood the signs, the words, the dreams."

But, how about all the times I prayed and saw the answers?

"Coincidence, my girl. Or, maybe God wanted those ones to happen. You don't always know what God is thinking, you know."

But, doesn't the bible say I have the mind of Christ?

"It's figurative, my darling. No one has the mind of Christ except Christ. Now, stop this silly roundabout journey. Just admit that it's possible that God didn't say."

That hit me like a bullet. No, it wasn't possible. There were too many signs. Too much had happened. God definitely said.

"Hmm, are you saying God is a liar? Because if He'd said it, wouldn't it have happened? And, yet, the same God gave the guy His blessing to propose to another girl. Come on, Omotayo, think about this."

I thought about it: God, the same God who had wooed me with His love, given me revelation of things I could never have known, spoken to me, led me, guided me. My God who was my Friend. He wouldn't do this to me. I must have misunderstood the words, misinterpreted the signs. He probably didn't say this guy was my husband.

"Good girl. Now, to show that you're mature and brave, and that you're not heartbroken because he moved on, call the guy and tell him that you realise God didn't say, and wish him well."

So I called him, put up the cheeriest voice I could muster without sounding plastic, said the equivalent of, "Whoops! Sorry I put you under all that pressure, I don't think God actually said anything. My bad."

He said he understood, we joked a bit and I got off the phone. Good man.

I did a summary video on my Instagram page to wrap the story up for anyone who was waiting for our wedding announcement. I hosted a hangout to encourage women who were waiting on a word, to tell them not to give up, and I planned to never speak about singleness, again.

I didn't notice when I had stopped praying, altogether. I fell into old, self-destructive habits. I wasn't able to encourage anyone in a waiting period; I couldn't say, "You know God won't fail you," because, even though I had "admitted" that God hadn't sent me on this journey, I still thought He was wicked to have let me go on it.

I felt guilty for thinking God was wicked, and I was angry that I still cared enough to feel guilty when He was the one who watched me use my own heart to play tennis without covering me.

I thought back to how much I had prayed, how earnestly I had sought His face for just this *one* thing, and He had led me into the valley of the shadow of disappointment.

Yet. I missed God so much. I wanted to make up with my Best Friend but I didn't know how we could ever get back to how it was before. He would probably just disappoint me again, then say it was a "lesson" or part of the "process". I hated those empty churchous words.

I was afraid that, if I continued like this, God would stop blessing me and the devil would start tormenting me, so I would say a sentence in the morning, "I declare that this is the day the Lord has made, I will rejoice and be glad in it." At night, it was, "Thank you for the day, Lord. Please help me sleep well and watch over me."

My journal was empty. I refused to write my dreams. I was struggling at work but I didn't know how to ask Him about anything, again. What if I assumed He was speaking but it wasn't actually Him? How could I trust Him to communicate with me, if He had watched me misunderstand but did nothing to correct me?

I was alone in the world. No one else understood, not really.

My two friends who God had told about their spouses had moved on: the one who'd been scared to speak ended up meeting her current husband two months after her heart was broken.

Two months after my heart was broken, it was still broken.

My other friend had started dating the guy God spoke to her about. It had worked out! They were committed and planning a future together.

But God had left me single and alone.

Blessings and Punishments

It is because we think God's blessings to us are our reward for good deeds, that we think our tough circumstances are His way of punishing us when we've done something wrong. So we try to figure out our flaws and mistakes, we work hard to be right before God so that bad things wouldn't happen. We try to dot all our i's and cross our t's so that when God comes like a strict teacher to check our work, He'll find us worthy.

Oh, but the heart of God is so full of love that there is no room for punishment in it. One of my favourite bible verses says this,

"There is no fear in love. But perfect love drives out fear, because fear has to do with punishment. The one who fears is not made perfect in love.

"We love because he first loved us." (1 John 4:18-19 NIV)

The Passion Translation puts it this way, "Love never brings fear, for fear is always related to punishment. But love's perfection drives the fear of punishment far from our hearts. Whoever walks constantly afraid of punishment has not reached love's perfection. Our love for others is our grateful response to the love God first demonstrated to us."

But we have questions:

"What's the point of serving God, then, since even the sinners get blessed?"

"Why have I been a good girl for all these years, when all the bad girls are getting the good guys?"

"What's the point of praying when bad things will still happen?"

"Since God will have mercy on whoever He chooses to have mercy on, I might as well do whatever I want."

"That woman has been serving God faithfully, but she's still single. What else does God want?!"

"How many years will I be in my waiting period before God decides that I deserve the answer to my prayer?"

Then there are the messages we hear that make God seem like a transactional and partial God:

"You don't have enough faith! God said that faith like a mustard seed can move mountains. Have you seen how tiny a mustard seed is? That means your own is even smaller, God cannot see your faith! You can never get your blessings if you don't have faith!"

"Prayer and fasting works. Jesus was in the wilderness for forty days, and the devil still tempted Him. You, you can't fast for one day and you want God to bless you?"

"Hmm, it's a pattern in your family. I see that your parents also struggled with this problem, and their parents, too. You need to break the cycle! You need deliverance!"

And on, and on.

I had gone for deliverance, fasted and prayed *and* I had faith that was bigger than a mustard seed, yet, I didn't get what I wanted. I got many other things – my car, my yellow bag, my new flat, a great job, good friends, freelance work, intimacy with God, peace of mind, surprise gifts, excellent health... my blessings are innumerable. But no husband, and no clarity of purpose.

"God is able to do anything! What you're asking for is so small, too small. God is saying, dream bigger! Those little dreams of yours are smaller than what God has for you!"

Well, that's confusing.

If my desires are so small that God is saying, "Ugh, a husband. Such a little thing. Money and career? Ugh, I scoff at money; I spit at career. Ask me for more!"

And, if it's the things I don't remember to ask for – like good health, safety and life – that He values more, then I actually don't need to pray for anything, because He'll only give me what He thinks is important.

Take a minute. Read that again.

If it's the things that we don't remember to ask for – like good health, safety and life – that He values more, then we actually don't need to pray for anything, because He'll only give us what He thinks is important.

Hmm.

Let's swap out, "what He thinks is important" with, "what He had already planned to give," because I'm not sure how important getting a yellow bag is, compared to good health.

Could it be, that God already knows all the blessings He wants to give everyone – and He will still give us those blessings, regardless of our good works or bad works?

If "He makes His sun rise on the evil and on the good, and sends rain on the just and on the unjust" (Matthew 5:45 NKJV), could it be that God is equally good to all human beings?

If He is, what's the point of choosing Christianity? Or even praying and being good? After all, the principles of success are the same, regardless.

Exactly: Choosing to believe in the sacrifice God made by coming to die for our sins is not something one just casually does, as if we're choosing one of the many different ways to worship God. It is the choice to believe in a God who, despite how unfathomably huge and endlessly powerful He is, chose to bend low, to look at His Creation face to face, so that they would feel how much He Loves them.

It is God in Heaven being interested in my makeup and clothing choices that makes me feel like I am valuable and special to Him.

It is God speaking to me and leading me, making jokes with me and loving me that shows me that He doesn't want to just be the distant God who blesses everyone; He wants to be the Loving God who becomes friends with the ones He created.

Some of us have fathers who were kind enough, but distant. We grow to respect and idolise them and that's fine – but some have fathers who play ball with them, take them to the salon, hug them when they come back from school, wipe their tears when they cry, call them when they travel, wait for them when they're out late. *They* grow to love their fathers, and that's amazing.

My father didn't need to be interested in the fact that I had broken up with the guy I was dating, but he was. My mother didn't need to cry, but she felt the pain. That is love.

And it is our ability to receive love that draws us to the only God who uses Love as His reason for existence, the only God who defines Himself as the epitome of Love. The only God who gives us His name and asks us to share in His identity, like a loving father does to his children, whom he loves.

Will He bless us, regardless? Yes.

Will He grant us favour at work? Absolutely.

Will He use us to change the world, whether we pray to Him or not? Without a doubt, the world is full of such men; just look at the advancements in science and technology, for a start.

But it is only when we learn how to receive His Love that we will experience the intimacy that comes with the bond between a Father and His child.

Recovery

I realised that God was still protecting me, even when I wasn't praying. I realised that He was still guiding me, leading me to make the right decisions. I realised that He was still... there. I couldn't be bad enough to shake Him off. I could feel Him with me when I cried on my way to work, or back home, or alone in my bed.

I moved from feeling guilty to being grateful.

"Thank You, Lord, that I can't shake You; that You love me more than I can imagine is possible."

It seemed that He meant what He'd said to me when I turned thirty; I really couldn't disappoint Him. He just kept on loving me right back into His good graces.

Then, one day, I got a nudge, "Omotayo, you said I didn't say what I said."

Panic hit. Just when I thought I couldn't disappoint God, here He was, telling me something I'd done wrong.

Before I even let Him explain, I rushed to apologise. "I'm sorry, I'm sorry!"

"Shh!" Stern.

I shushed.

"Omotayo, because it didn't work out the way you thought it would, you said I didn't say what I said."

He was talking about the guy.

"B-but-"

"But, what?"

I was confused.

"Omotayo. Do I speak to you?"

Yes, Lord.

"How many things have I told you that have proven to be true?"

The very many things ran through my mind.

"And yet, because one thing didn't go according to your plan, you said I didn't say what I said."

I started crying. "I'm sorry, L-"

"Shh!" Like a Parent scolding a crying child, saying, "Come on, will you stop crying. You broke the toy and now you're crying. Come on, keep quiet and pay attention as I scold you back to your senses."

Again, "You said I didn't say what I said."

God played back every word, every dream, every confirmation. He reminded me that He had also showed me that the guy was going to propose to someone else. If that part had happened in real life, how could I dismiss every other thing? How could I pick and choose what to believe to suit my feelings? What kind of relationship did I think this was, since when was God's word only valid in the good times, and irrelevant in the bad?

God showed me that I've had a misplaced understanding of consequences and punishment, an erroneous concept of time, a faulty idea of good and evil. He was trying to explain that He also doesn't "allow" bad things to teach us lessons or take us through "a learning process." God doesn't use pain or hurt to teach, He uses love.

Ah, I wept.

See, God can choose Love – not just because He *is* love – but because He has seen the entirety of time from the end to the beginning and back again. He has no reason to be angry with us, or to be impatient and judgmental, because He already knows everything that's going to happen.

Our weaknesses don't surprise Him; our failures don't shock Him.

He knows the timing of our lives: how long we will spend in each season, how many years we will live, how many friends we will have, how many times we will feel pain.

He uses our mistakes and misfortunes to create dramatic plot twists that take us right back to the path we were always supposed to be on, in the first place.

And so, we are never "waiting" and we can't "miss it". God is always working and weaving the paths of our lives together to create a beautiful, intricate tapestry.

There is no "waiting season," there is only life.

A child is not waiting to be an adult; children are not incomplete because they haven't grown up. They're just living and growing.

A tree is not waiting to be made into a table; it is not lacking or flawed because it hasn't been made into a shelf. It is just a tree. And when the day comes for it to be cut down, it will then go on the process of becoming a table. But whether or not it becomes a table, it is still a fully valuable tree.

I'm not waiting for God to decide that I've suffered enough to finally deserve marriage; He is not "holding back my husband", either – it's just not yet time.

The desire has been stirred: He has taken me, the rib, out of my Adam and He is forming and fashioning me into Woman and leading me to him. How long will it take? I don't know; it doesn't matter. Adam and Eve lived in a timeless Garden so we don't know how long it took for God to fashion Eve into her identity as a wife, or how long it took for God to lead her to Adam.

The problem with living as if you're constantly waiting for something is this: the longer it takes, the more discouraged you feel. The more you start to think there must be something wrong with you, and the more you struggle to try to work to be better, act better, think better, pray better. And when you see others who don't pray half as much as you do getting everything you've

179

prayed for, you think God is being unfair. That's what it means when the Bible says, "hope deferred makes the heart sick." (Proverbs 13:12) God doesn't want our hearts to be sick, that's not the reason why He sends Hope. He stirs us up to prepare us for the blessing He's bringing, not to make us so sick with longing that we become discouraged.

He never sent you on that wild goose chase, running up and down from deliverance pastor to prayer camp, looking for breakthrough. He wanted to draw you closer to Him in intimacy and fellowship, preparing you from the inside. We must learn to "name the animals" in the time of preparation, like Adam did, so that we'll recognise the fulfilment of our desires when it happens.

On this journey, I have learnt how to be a better friend. I have learnt how to forgive. I have learnt how to be courageous, to run after God in faith even when it looks foolish. I am learning that these are the attributes of God: He is the Best Friend. He has forgiven us eternally. He runs after us with His fierce Love –

– But God did not "make me single" so that I could learn these lessons, He taught me these lessons because I was single and waiting. Instead of living and making the most of each day, I was pining for a future that I had no control over. I could have learnt to love and trust God without the pain of heartache and disappointment.

In every season, Single or Married, God wants us to live full and complete lives. He wants us to live abundant lives, abundant in health, in peace, in love.

Because, when it all comes down to it, the purpose of our lives is to reflect a unique aspect of His nature.

How To Be Single

The first time I ever talked about Singleness in an intentional way, my friend, Bolatito, had been interviewing me on her talk show and the director spontaneously asked me to give five tips on How to be Single. I came up with these points:

- Love yourself, flaws and all.
- Know your identity.
- Have good friends.
- Have clear values.
- Ladies, look for a guy who has close male friends and/or mentors that he can confide in and be accountable to.

By the time I was doing my first live chat, I had forgotten the last two points and reshuffled the list to read:

- Value yourself.
- Be honest with yourself about what you want; stop pretending that you're happy being single if you really want to be in a committed relationship.
- Fix your flaws. Don't hide your bad behavior under the guise of personality. That's *not* "just how you are".

- Have good friends.
- Know God for yourself.

If we merge both lists, we have:
- Value yourself, flaws and all.
- Be intentional about improving yourself. Don't hide bad behavior under the guise of personality; that's *not* "just how you are".
- Know God for yourself – and know your identity in God.
- Have clear values.
- Have good friends.
- Forgive – your parents, your exes, yourself.
- Stop waiting to get married before you achieve your dreams; live your life to the fullest.

Let's discuss each of the seven points:

1. Value yourself, flaws and all:

We weren't born feeling flawed; we learnt to question ourselves as we grew up. We call it maturity, but it is conformity: pressure to be and to do what you *think* the people around you want you to do and be.

One day, after years of being unhappy about my belly fat, complaining about my figure and wishing I had a bigger bum, I realised something: Even when I was eighteen years old and my waist was only 27 inches, I had been complaining about my figure. At what point would I accept that I was alright the way I was? At what point would I be good enough for me?

Because I didn't like my bum, I didn't dance confidently. Because I didn't like my stomach, I wore clothes that were a size bigger and pretended that it was just my personal style. Because I didn't like my edges, I wore wigs.

And don't we all do that? We make choices to cover our flaws and act like it's normal, but then when we're in relationships we get scared of our partners seeing us just as we are because, what if they also don't like us, just as we are?

So we try to be sexier, richer, cooler, better, widely read, well travelled, a deeper Christian, bible scholar, etc etc etc. There's nothing wrong with any of these things, in and of themselves, but if we're doing them just to make others like and value us, we'll find ourselves constantly frustrated with the world when things don't work out the way we think they should.

And yet, haven't you ever seen someone who looked completely different from you – thicker waist, bigger bum, smaller bank account, less accomplished career, never goes to church, doesn't live in your kind of neighbourhood – who looked so much happier and more content than you? That's because our looks don't define us. Our wallets don't define us. Our achievements don't define us. Our religious activities don't define us.

Contentment is an internal process that has external benefits, but we can't use external achievements to create internal contentment.

I have tried to use both surface examples and deep examples to show that *anything* can affect our feeling of value and self worth. It's not always the "big" things; it's not always the "serious" things. And, sometimes, it is the seemingly silly things that give us permission to take a step toward recovering our sense of value.

For some people, it was abuse that stole our confidence. For others, it was just life – the opinions of other people who lashed out at us because they didn't value themselves ended up sticking, until we reduced our value to fit within the box of their words.

But that's not what God intended.

When we allow ourselves to believe that we are valuable, just as we are, then we will truly be on our way to living whole lives: perfect and complete, lacking nothing.

2. Be intentional about improving yourself:

Don't hide bad character under the guise of "that's just who I am".

The fact that you love yourself doesn't mean that you're perfect.

One example is with romantic relationships. If you've ever been in love, you know what it's like to absolutely love someone – even though they do some things that annoy you.

Another easy example is a mother's love for her child: the fact that the child is absolutely and entirely loved doesn't mean the child isn't naughty and rebellious, sometimes. The child still has to be taught and trained.

But there's a difference between when a mother trains her child out of love and when a harsh teacher punishes a pupil out of anger.

In love, a mother corrects and points her child to the right way. Through her actions, she's saying, "Look, you're a good child. This naughty behaviour is not who you are." She reaffirms the child's value even as she corrects the behaviour.

In anger, a harsh teacher condemns the child by emphasising their bad behaviour. "You're a naughty child. I'm punishing you to let you know how naughty you are."

The mother corrects her child's bad behaviour and reminds him/her of his/her value.

The harsh teacher punishes bad behaviour in a way that makes the child feel like they have lost their value because of their actions.

If you learn to see yourself as someone who's worthy of love, you'll realise that you can love yourself and still recognise that there are character traits that you need to fix.

I have many character weaknesses. As we say, God is working on me, and I am intentionally allowing Him to do so.

A huge one was when He started teaching me about respecting my brothers. Listen – I'd never thought of myself as disrespectful, but I also never thought of my brothers as being worthy of my respect. As far as I was concerned, we were all equals as long as we were siblings. What made it worse was that I considered the age difference between us to be negligible. Ha!

Once, when we were still in university, my eldest brother was so mad at me that he told me not to go out.

What??

I could feel the figurative smoke coming out of my ears. I went out, anyway, and he called the driver and told him to bring the car back home – while I was out. And it was raining.

I got down in the rain, as the driver mumbled an awkward apology and drove home. I took a taxi with my friend and swore to myself to show him even more "pepper". Nonsense.

But, years later, I was on this journey of being who God wanted me to be and I found myself the object of my brothers' collective disapproval. My second eldest brother had asked me to sweep.

To sweep, me! Why should I sweep?

He yelled at me, saying I didn't contribute any value to the house – financially, or otherwise. That stung! I wasn't earning money and was already feeling unworthy and then he added my inability to contribute to the bills to make it even worse.

Later, at what was supposed to be a bonding sibling hangout, the other brothers gathered together to point out that I'd always had an attitude.

One said, "It's not like I have a problem with you, or anything, I'm just worried about you being able to add value when you get married, too."

Ouch.

I cried so much when I got home. I felt attacked by my brothers, and I felt betrayed by God.

"Lord," I wept, "If I truly had such a terrible character defect, why didn't You tell me, Yourself? Why shame me in front of my brothers like that? If You had told me in private, I would have changed!"

Truth is, probably not; I'm more likely to have argued than conformed.

I didn't know what to do different. I had a sense that the issue wasn't really the sweeping or the bills; it was my attitude of general aloofness and detachment. In fact,

I took pride in not caring about anything and I knew it was annoying.

I started trying to practice showing concern, being kind, and being warm and friendly to my brothers. I already had practice being kind to other people I wasn't related to, but I didn't bring any of that growth and maturity home.

So, my brother would come home from work and I would say, "How are you? How was work?" then I would actually listen.

Or I would have an issue, perhaps a question I'd been mulling over or a theory I was forming and I'd go to them, "What do you think about this? What is your opinion?" And I would actually listen. Not to argue, to prove my point or to win, but to genuinely hear what they had to say.

I'm still not the best at this, but I now see the men in my life as genuinely valuable parts of my life and I have grown to respect them, whether or not I agree with them.

It was only along the line that God explained to me that this was just a shadow of what respecting and submitting to a husband looked like.

3. Learn to know God for yourself – and find out your true identity in God.

I used to think God was like a benevolent Monarch, a kind King; He's kind and considerate of His people, but you can't come close to Him. I used to think that God had a list of rules and regulations and, even though He could be nice, He could throw you into His dungeon if you broke any of His rules. I used to think that the only people God was interested in talking to were ordained clergymen. I used to think that I had to fast and pray and read my bible consistently for a long period of time before I could get God to respond to my prayers. I used to think that the bible was a boring book we were forced to read so that God would be happy with us; I never thought I would be able to understand the mysterious ideas the bible expressed. I used to think that I had to be kneeling down and closing my eyes before I could pray; if my eyes were open I could be struck blind.

I could go on.

But, on my journey with God, I learnt that God hears the whispers of my heart. I learnt that God understands my sighs. I found out that God has a sense of humour and He loves to share jokes with us. I learnt that I could be driving in traffic and communing with Him; that He cared about what I wore, how I dressed and how I did my hair. I learnt that God was interested in helping me be a good friend, that He cared when my heart was broken, that He didn't accuse or condemn me for my wrongdoing; He only corrected me and redirected me to the right path.

I learnt all of this by myself: God led me to like-minded people who were struggling with similar temptations – lust, drinking, clubbing – but who still really wanted to find God. I listened to sermons by younger pastors who dressed cool and talked with slangs, because they sounded like me and they talked about things that I was struggling with. I listened to my audio bible so that I could hear it even when I didn't have the attention span to read it. And when I heard things that confused me or annoyed me, I took it to my small fellowship groups and I asked questions. And, gradually, I learnt that I could ask God, Himself.

Learning God for myself, outside the confines of a traditional Church setting, gave me the freedom to explore, stumble and watch God catch me.

I started to see myself the way God saw me. The bible says, "As Christ is, so are we on the earth." (1 John 4:17) I started to understand that God meant it literally when He said, "Don't you know that ye are gods?" (John 10:34), and that He truly meant for me to be able to do what Jesus did when He was on the earth – and even more (John 14:12).

These literal promises were pieces of the picture of who God is, and who God created me to be. That formed the foundation of my identity and gave me a new confidence: I learnt that I am the beloved of the Lord. The more I look at Him and understand His nature, the more I understand what my true nature is meant to be. And the more I imitate Him, the more I become like Him. His Word is a mirror that reflects my true personality to me (2 Corinthians 3:18).

When we learn to know God for ourselves, we grow into our true identity.

We are not what the world has said about us, we are not our mistakes, we are not our pasts. We are the beloved of the Lord, we are joint heirs with Him! We are His workmanship, He created us to fulfil the dreams and plans He had before our parents even knew they were going to get together and give birth to us.

This identity of love, of our immense value to God – this is what drowns out the lies, the insecurities; the "who do you think you are", the "you'll never be able to achieve that, stop dreaming." Because if you are from God and made of God to be like God, then you can also do all things through God who strengthens you.

4. Have Clear Values

We all know Christians who turn up on Saturday night at the club, get to church hung-over but still lift holy hands during praise and worship (and always make sure they pay their tithes and offerings), single Christian guys who suit up to serve as ushers but are sleeping with the choir members, billionaires who got their fortunes illegally but believe they can sow enough seeds to buy God's pardon – these are examples of Christians who don't have clear values.

Again, your right behaviour does not qualify you for more blessings but, my fellow singles, they qualify you for peace of mind – and help you discern who has honourable intentions for you from who doesn't.

Try this, tell the next person you're dating that you don't want to have sex before marriage and see how they respond. Some will pretend to be fine with it and still try to seduce you. Some will walk away immediately. Either way, drawing a clear line like that will help you see who is likely to commit and who isn't interested in making long-term plans.

5. Have Good Friends

If it hadn't been for my friends, I would not have survived being single for so long. Singleness can be really lonely; you want to go to the cinema but have no one to go with. You want to go dancing, but there's no one to dance with. Because I had good friends, I was never alone. Apart from physical desires, I never had to be lonely.

I had friends who went partying with me, friends I confided my deep secrets and fears to, friends I prayed with, friends I worked with. Every area of my life was covered.

But many people don't have good friends; some have been betrayed by old friends and some just don't know how to make friends. The simple rule is this: if you want a good friend, be a good friend.

Being a good friend means being vulnerable first. Don't wait for the other person to spill their secrets before you spill yours; vulnerability is what creates bonds. If you're worried about giving too much away, too quickly, then start by sharing things you have in common. That's a good starting point.

Being a good friend also means learning how to forgive. Think about it, you're upset that someone "shared your gist", but haven't you ever shared someone else's gist? The fact that you said, "don't tell anyone" and that you denied it when you were confronted about it does not mean you haven't done it.

I've fought with many of my friends – some fights lasted years! But for the most part, we were able to forgive each other and become even closer than we were before. Not just that fake forgiveness where you pretend to be over it just to appear "mature" – we've had real, sensitive, sometimes petty fights where we let the other person know exactly how much we were hurt without being afraid that one person would dismiss the other's feelings.

Fighting isn't pleasant, but making up makes you closer. I used to dream of having friends who "knew me better than I knew myself", like on *Sex and the City*. I realised, first, that TV is not real life; but I also realised that deep friendships come with deep commitment and an even deeper ability to be vulnerable, honour each other, and always, *always* forgive.

If you're wondering whether you need to forgive *that* friend, the answer is probably yes.

If you're wondering how to know the difference between toxic friendships, seasonal friendships and friends who just need to be forgiven, the answer is that you can only find out after you have forgiven them over and over again. A toxic friend is likely to disregard your feelings or keep trying to make you feel guilty even after you're supposed to have moved past it. Seasonal friends tend to drift away without any fight or drama. Lifetime friends may hurt your feelings the deepest, but you'll miss each other terribly and you'll both be so happy to be friends again, after you've made up.

6. Forgive.

Sis! Bro! Come; take a seat.

Look, forgive your parents. It doesn't matter whether they did it intentionally or whether they had good intentions, they still ended up hurting you. Some of the things they said have scarred you; you still remember when your mum said that thing and you've always wondered if you were really a useless, good for nothing child.

And now, when you get in trouble at work or when a friend calls you out for doing something wrong, you react badly because it brings back memories of when your dad said he was disappointed in you.

You spend your energy trying to work hard enough to show them that you are good enough; that you are worthy of their love and approval, but they don't seem to notice. They don't seem to care. They just tell you about someone else's children and how *they* are doing wonderful things.

It hurts, but you have learnt to make jokes about it, dismiss it and act like you don't care; you tell yourself, "it was so long ago! Of course you're not still hurt." But you are. Their words cut deep – and they still do. You're still a little afraid of disappointing them and you still worry that they'll reject you if you don't live your life by their rules.

Take a deep breath –

Picture your mum, your dad. Maybe your step-mum or step-dad. Bring your uncle in – that uncle, yes. And that aunt who treated you badly. Bring your lesson teacher in, your driver, your friend's parents, the principal who told you you were never going to amount to anything. Your ex, his friends who lied to your face. His mum, too. Bring them all into the picture.

In your mind, tell them what they did. Tell them how it hurt. Tell them how you've lived your life afraid that what they said and did would define you. Tell them how you now know that they were wrong; that you are not defined by what happened.

– now let it out; let it all out, and forgive them.

You're going to be okay.

7. Stop Waiting.

Stop waiting to get married before you achieve your dreams. Stop living in your imagination. Stop closing your eyes, imagining what you would do, if only…

You are whole, perfect and complete, lacking nothing. You have everything inside you to do every great thing you desire to do. You can make a lot of money, travel the world – or you can start a company. You can teach, if you like, or start a crèche. You can serve in church and go on evangelical missions if that's what you desire to do. You don't have to reduce the size of your life to fit the size of your fears. The fact that you're not in a relationship doesn't mean you're not qualified to live.

Experiment, make mistakes, then pick yourself up and try again.

You were made out of the breath of the Living God, so, Live. Live your life to the fullest.

My hope is that you have been able to see how I picked up each of these lessons on my journey, and that you are able to apply them to yours.

Living Free

The very first thing I ever wanted to be was a writer. It is through words that I see the world; I'm always turning them over in my mind, wondering what they mean, playing with them, analysing them, wanting to speak them, act them, draw them, visualise them. I was made out of the Word and I have always needed to express the Word, myself – but all my life, I just wanted to be normal. "Normal" meant that all the things I was most passionate about would be my hobbies, and that I would find a steady job, build a career, get married early and live a life that would make my family not have to worry about me. Maybe I would even have extra to give them, on top of it.

It has taken me almost thirty-four years to realise that I am not normal; I am extraordinary. I am a conduit of the Most High and so it is impossible to be normal, to blend in. My light has been seeping out through the cracks that formed every time my heart was broken by a false expectation because God has been trying to break me free of the mask of approval and normalcy that I craved so desperately.

I spent my life looking for love and all the while, I'd already had it. My eternal connection to God, the

Source of Love, was in my ability to embrace the dream He had moulded me around.

Singleness has been the biggest and most important lesson of my life; the understanding that I am whole in myself and, while there is always room to build character, strengthen values and grow in courage, I am enough, truly enough – not because I am a woman or I am a goddess but because I was made from the fabric of God, Himself. This is no Beyoncé rhetoric; this is Gospel:

As Christ was, so am I on the earth. He has given me authority and power to call on Heaven to influence change on earth. I am a world changer because I have been supernaturally empowered to do so, and my current preoccupation is staring these truths in the eye and repeating them over and over until I am deeply rooted in this Love who chose to share Divinity with me.

I still wonder what happened with the guy I thought I would marry. I still meet new people and wonder, "Could it be him?" I still have all the physical desires – and I still subject them to the understanding that it is not time, so help me, God. (The fear of heartbreak is the beginning of self-control!)

I still wonder if I'm too old to still have four (or five) children, I wonder whether the men left over are leftovers as in the Yoruba, "ajeku", or "remnants" the way the Bible describes them (the best, saved for last). I still call my friends and whine about how I really *really* wanted a certain spec, *o*, and would I have to give it up now that I'm old?

I still wonder if God has a rich sheik in store for me somewhere, so that I can live this creative life without ever worrying about bills. I wonder exactly how this book will get as far as the ends of the earth. I still wonder what my parents and uncles will think when they read it – I still worry about coming across too militantly Jesus, sometimes.

I still breathe air, I am still single and I am still a human being – except that now, I understand that I am a human being God. And in that, whether I am single or married, I am whole, perfect and complete, lacking nothing.

Acknowledgments

I'm so thankful for this journey. Everyone who has been in my life for the last ten years is such a critical part of my growth and it will be impossible to acknowledge you all, but I will try.

I'd like to thank my dad for giving me the words that started me off. You still owe me the balance of everyone else's school fees, sha.

Mummy, don't worry! I'm going to be alright.

Zulu'mo! Nwanne'm. My constant. My words for you go beyond this ten-year journey so I will just say I love you for being my friend in this, and in every other single thing.

I'd like to thank my one and only Esther for being my sister for the first half of this journey of faith and finding love. I love talking about how we went from clubbing to bible study together! Having you as my friend through that transition was God's gift to me and I will always love you.

Omilola, I love you so much! Thank you for giving me the opportunity to serve. I will never forget seeing you from a distance in church and marveling at your freedom to just worship! Your intimacy with God inspired me, and your courage gave me courage to go out on a limb for God regardless of the world's opinions.

You have taught me so much just by letting me watch you. Thank you for letting me edit your book! Thank you for trusting me. And thank you for being my sister.

Funmi (Rotimi) Olaifa. I'm so thankful that we became friends again after you exed me for over five years. Listen, girl, I love you. You are such an amazing writer (who writes a good first draft? WHO?) Release the book(s), already.

Tolaaaa, the one I bought an engagement ring for! Need I say more? I love the fact that you are my friend. I am always in your corner.

Irene my ore, the multi-talented, the amazing, the beautiful. I really admire you, Irene. You braved the pressure in this critical world of ours and embraced a fulltime career as an illustrator! You're proof that fear is just an illusion. I love you!

Odunayo! We'll still write the book about our story. I'm so proud of you for trusting God to the very end. I'm so happy to see how happy you are. Thank you for being my number one confidant when we entered into the crazy season. Thank you for your dreams, prayers, arguments and fights and love. You are my friend and I love you.

Shout out Oluwatobiloba and Nifs! Thank you for everything, sisters. And Precious! Thank you for allowing me to turn our business meeting into a faith session. Special shout out to Afolake Olawuyi – you were the first one to show me that it was possible to hear God and not see it but still trust Him fully. (Isn't it time for us to get back together, yet?)

To Girl – Oby, Toks, Fati, Tolu, Irene, Zu – you guys are the friends I think about when I talk about having good friends. You never made me feel like the odd single friend, you were open and real about marriage and you were quietly hopeful that I would get there, too. I'll still get there, o! I appreciate you.

Moradeke my wife! Ify! Rolake! Amakaaa! I love you! Sneaky shout out to my teacher-friends, Simi and Tolu – you made teaching less difficult. And thank you for following your dreams! I'm so proud of you!

Bolatito! You are Royalty! Thank you for living life in the open even when there are so many contrary voices. You're so beautiful.

The Abba's Jewels! Love you, ladies! Ivie mama, thank you so much for all your love – it just pours out of you and I receive it. Love you!

Ayodipupo! Adeolu! Oyakhire! My brothers, my brothers! I love you guys so much. I'm so proud to famz with you. Thank you for being such great friends, thank you for always listening to me, thank you for tolerating my aunty behavior, thank you for praying with me and for me. Thank you for being my brothers!

Thank you so much, Sola Adeola. You are such a pivotal part of my faith journey, you can't imagine. Thank you for that day when you told me your story and added me to a random email thread. Thank you for gifting me with Sozo. Thank you for always being there, even from a distance. Ogochukwu! Thank you for our annual catchups. Thank you for encouraging me to write my list. Thank you for Hosting the Presence!

Burning Bush and Momentum Networks! You guys changed my life. Thank you, Toyin Olubake for being such a great gatherer.

GLA + Ignite! My family. Thank you for being home. Thank you for all the opportunities to serve. Pastor Wale and Pastor Laolu, thank you for leaving the doors of your home open to me, for the constant lunches, for the opportunity to work at GLA, for your visionary leadership and family love. PB, PM, EA, I appreciate you. Pastor and Prophetess Dami and Dupe! Thank you for your courage, for your light and for salt.

Thank you, Ronke, Tomi, Teni for having the courage to follow your own paths. Watching you encouraged me to try, too. Fingers crossed we all end up truly rich – in life and in love. Shout out to Eniola and Bolaji for being the first of us to give our parents the satisfaction!

Olaolu! Debola! Gboyega! Doyin – my brothers, the first men in my life. Thank you for being men-men-men-men-Manly-men-men-men. Love you! (Seye you're in here, too. Thank you for always being there. I really appreciate you). Thank you to (some of) the other men who were part of this story. I wish I could shout some of you out but it would be so weird. thnks fr the mmrs.

I'm sure I'll remember someone else I missed out and feel terrible and have to apologise in person. Please forgive me in advance.

Even though this is the end, it's also just the beginning and I thank You, Lord, for everything.

About the Author

OMOTAYO ADEOLA is Firecatcher: a Light that helps others find their own Light. She works as a Writer, Producer and Content Creator, and has experience in film, TV, radio, advertising, fashion, education, art and digital marketing.

Omotayo studied English at the University of Lagos and has a Masters in Writing from the University of Warwick, for which she bagged a Distinction.

"How To Be Single" is her first published book.

)

Printed in Great Britain
by Amazon

55672889R00120